Don't Be Dumb

A Leadership Playbook to Help You Be Smarter, Overcome Obstacles, and Rise Rapidly in Challenging Times

ROBERT TOWLE

PRAISE FOR *DON'T BE DUMB*

Robert led his team, engaging with three major universities, and developed strong recommendations. These included several improvements and savings that went beyond the hired scope of services and added significant value to our stakeholders. I'm confident his real-life experiences in this book will help others do the same in their organizations.
—Mark J. Braun, Executive Director, Board of Regents, State of Iowa

Robert and I worked together developing and giving seminars to franchisees to help them drive their business to the next level. I'm excited to see that he's put his experiences into a book to help other professionals in both the private and public sectors.
—Bob Mermelstein, Non-Profit Financial Consultant

Robert brings forth his wealth of experiences via a collection of unique, yet intertwined, stories of his life—both personal and professional. He does so in a manner that is informative, from a "lessons learned" perspective, and is real world and humorous. This is the business version of "everything i needed to know I learned in kindergarten." It's practical, useful, and encouraging.
—Jeff Gosline, Senior Director, Customer Development, DHL Supply Chain

I've seen Robert's work up close through his participation in the Shared Services Leadership Coalition, including his insightful testimony on the value proposition of shared services to a subcommittee of the US House of Representatives. This book puts his distinctive leadership

experience to work, helping other professionals move forward in their careers and in their life journeys.
—John Marshall, Founder and CEO,
Shared Services Leadership Coalition

Robert worked for me for several years. His thoughts in this book on approaching leadership and overcoming obstacles in the workplace are a great fit for addressing the challenges that we face in organizations today.
—Mike Rescoe, Board Member, Darling Ingredients, Inc. and Previous Board Member with Global Crossing and Global Power Equipment Group

Robert and his team used a great approach to help my former organization grow to the next level. His thoughts in this book will help people at all levels in their organization apply unique ideas to challenging situations.
—Ann-Marie Massenberg, Former Client

Robert led a team that helped my organization reorganize, improve processes, and cut costs in Europe. Across all levels of someone's career, I can see the real-life experiences of a seasoned professional shared in this book helping them to identify and overcome obstacles as well as when to just "let go" on their way to greater success.
—Chris Newman, Vice-President, Finance—Fiserv

The topics in this book fit examples of workshops I've brought Robert in to give through the last years. His knowledge has always left attendees with more information, as will the roadmap of ideas he is offering in the book.
—Jules Miller, President & Executive Producer,
Insight Council

I worked with Robert as a client a couple of years ago and appreciate that he's put his ideas into a book for other professionals. These insights will help people at all levels of their career.
—Brenda Rebman, MBA, CPHR, CMC, CHE, President, Futures Resource Partners Inc.

Robert and his team helped our organization create a strong foundation and action plans that we have built upon over the years. The insights he's put in his book will be of great assistance in helping businesspeople at all levels in their careers.
—Mike Riccio, Chief Financial Officer and Treasurer of Panasonic Corporation of North America (PNA)

I've known Robert for more than 25 years. His insight and guidance were instrumental in the early success of my company. This book provides the same nuggets that Robert shared with us that helped Firespring become chosen as one of America's 50 Best Workplaces by *Inc. Magazine*. There are many lessons to be discovered here, and I believe that everyone in business should read this book.
—Jay Wilkinson, Founder of Firespring and Founder of the Do More Good Movement

This book offers stories that apply beyond business situations, providing insights to a broad range of subjects. The stories draw one in, like binge-watching episode after episode of a television series. Valuable insights for improvement will assist you regardless of your role or stage of your career.
—Rob Rowan, author of *Foreign Currency Financial Reporting* and Former Client

I've worked with Robert over the past 15+ years, and I've always found his advice, based on his varied experience, to be the help I needed. And his book, *Don't Be Dumb*, is a perfect example of this. Great learning for those younger and a great reminder for those a bit older.
—Tom Nash, Chief Procurement Officer, American Red Cross

Don't Be Dumb

*A Leadership Playbook to
Help You Be Smarter,
Overcome Obstacles, and Rise
Rapidly in Challenging Times*

ROBERT TOWLE

Don't Be Dumb © 2021 by Robert M. Towle. All rights reserved.

Published by Author Academy Elite
PO Box 43, Powell, OH 43065
www.AuthorAcademyElite.com

All rights reserved. This book contains material protected under International and Federal Copyright Laws and Treaties. Any unauthorized reprint or use of this material is prohibited. No part of this book may be reproduced or transmitted in any form or by any means, electronic or mechanical, including photocopying, recording, or by any information storage and retrieval system, without express written permission from the author.

Identifiers:
LCCN: 2021908839
ISBN: 978-1-64746-798-2 (paperback)
ISBN: 978-1-64746-799-9 (hardback)
ISBN: 978-1-64746-800-2 (ebook)

Available in paperback, hardback, and e-book

Any Internet addresses (websites, blogs, etc.) and telephone numbers printed in this book are offered as a resource. They are not intended in any way to be or imply an endorsement by Author Academy Elite, nor does Author Academy Elite vouch for the content of these sites and numbers for the life of this book.

Some names and identifying details have been changed to protect the privacy of individuals.

Dedication

To my dad, who first gave the advice of "don't be dumb" over the breakfast table while I was in junior high. Although Mom wanted him to give me a cheerier piece of advice, it runs through my head and helps me every day.

To my mom, whose support in teaching me to play piano (and practicing daily) not only taught me to work harder to correct mistakes (or "klinkers", in her terminology), but likely saved me from tragic consequences from the brain tumor that was discovered in my frontal lobe in 2018.

Additional thanks to my wife, Catherine, my boys, Evan and Brice, family and friends for their continued support and advice.

TABLE OF CONTENTS

"Seeing the Elephant"—An Introduction 1

Leadership, Not Management 7

   Don't Focus on the "Green Grass of Kentucky" . .9
      The Alps in Switzerland 9
      You Snuck on My Blindside While
         I Was Shuckin' These Peas! 10
      My First Real Job! 11
      Train Yourself to Look Forward 12

   If You Leave Late, It Just Gets Later and Later . .13
      Consensus Management—Delays 13
      Squirrels Chasing Shiny Objects 14
      Ronnie the Entrepreneur. 15
      A Lot of Shoes at Christmas 17
      Why That Mountain? What Should We Pack? . . .19
      Rapidly Get on "The Road" 19

   You Get What You Need 21
      I Can't Live on What I'm Worth 21
      Pay Me to Drive It Off the Lot 22
      Get What You Need .23

   Don't Blindfold Your Boss 24
      Transparency Is a Frightening Thing 24
      The Russians Are Going to Invade! 25
      The Project Manager Was Arrested 26
      Removing the Blindfold 28

Don't Believe Your Own Press Clippings 30
    The Manager Walk 31
    I Am an Officer's Wife! 32
    Long Live the King! 33
    Being Humble as a Leader. 35

HR Tips That HR Might Not Approve Of 37

    Sometimes It's iHop Time! 39
        But She Isn't a Witch! .39
        2 + 2 Doesn't Equal 5. 40
        The Pinkerton Vanishing Act. 43
        The Pleasure of the Governor. 43
        Congratulations on Your Demotion 44
        The Captain Is Unconscious on His Desk. 46
        iHop Time. 47
        The Golden Canary and Rehydrated Peaches. .48
        How Dare You Spend $150! 49
        Saying Goodbye to Hollywood 50

    Being "Already Gone" at Work 52
        Stick to Your Word 52
        The Semi-Annual Employee Purge 54
        No Laissez-Faire with Layoffs. 56

    Go Be Happy Somewhere Else 58
        My Grandfather Is in the Hospital! 59
        I Know How to Use a Gun! 60
        Does He Know He's Been Fired? 61
        Bend Over and Untie Your Boots 64
        Checking out of the Marriott. 65
        No Help Needed 66
        Help Guide Them to Their Happy. 67

    The FISH Principle 69
        What Water? 69
        Tucson Toro's Spring Training. 70
        The Financial Weather Report 71

    Sock-Em Boppers 71
    Everyone, Please Celebrate Me! 72
    The FISH Principle 73
    Making FISH Work for You! 76

Improving the Work in the *Work*place 77

You'll End up Just Like Ricky the Goat! 79
    My First Real Job! 79
    Zero-Basing 80
    Leaning toward Sawyer's 81
    Don't Be Like Ricky! 83
    Warning: Don't Do It! 85
    Avoiding Barbwire Fences 86

**Work Until Your Work Reaches
Its Logical Conclusion** 88
    The Logical Conclusion of Your Work 88
    How Many Name Changes Are Enough? 90
    I Don't Know Their Name! 91
    Two Men out and Three on Base 91

Mistake-Proofing 93
    Stuck at an Airport 93
    Sandwich Shop, Baskets, and Trash Cans 94
    How to Mistake-Proof 95

Don't Be Dumb 96
    Eliminate S.T.U.P.I.D. 96
    How to Eliminate S.T.U.P.I.D.: 99

**Bring on the Dynamite! —Removing Obstacles
at Work** 101

Maintain the Bungee-Cord Approach 103
    It's Bus Time 103
    New Computers via the Rental Car Express . .104
    Rebuilding the Cubicles 105
    I'll See You in the Office Tomorrow 106

Zero to Worry about in Payroll 107
The Last-Minute Sri Lankan Tourist. 108
Avoiding Quicksand. .109

Bring Me a Calculator!. .110
Rockingham as a Secret Code. 110
Don't Ignore Old Methods 112
Get the Shelves out of the Basement 113
Using Flint and Steel .114

Don't Fall for the Chaff. .116
$49,900 in the Suitcase 117
Rock Collections and M&Ms. 118
Arm Wrestling over a Simple Agreement 119
How to Ignore the *Chaff* 120

Recovering from the Irrecoverable Spin 121
The Elevator Ate My Keys. 121
The Old Gas Stove. .122
Go Call the Police—I'll Stall Them! 124
Don't Forget to Breathe! 125
The Worst Conference Call in the
　　History of the Universe 127
Pulling up to Better Results 128

Finding Good in Bad Situations 130
The Best Half-Concert Ever 130
Miami Vice Was a Long Time Ago 133
The Great Escape 134
The Art of Truck Tackling 137
Escaping the Maze. .138

Rise More Rapidly 139

Buy the Utensils. 141
The Admin Assistant as HR Head? 141
Sicker than a Dog in Iowa 142
Why Did I Take This Job? 143
Overachievement Is OK 144

Keep Going If You Know You're Right 147
    Ignore the Experts (Sometimes) 147
    The Weird Enron Field Investment 149
    Be the Kool-Aid Pitcher! 150

Go and Grab Your Cape! 153
    I Am Not Qualified for the Role 153
    Legally Blind Accountant—Rising Rapidly . . . 155
    Nope—Not Qualified for This One Either! 156
    The Lion of the Round Top 157
    Saving Lives in Hong Kong? 159
    Burn the Ships 160

Time to Fly! 161

Appendix 165
    Project Plan Example 165
    Project Stakeholder Chart (Sample) 166
    Project Role Definitions (Sample) 167
    Weekly Project Update Example 170
    S.T.U.P.I.D. Sighting Report 171

Endnotes 173

About the Author 177

"SEEING THE ELEPHANT"— AN INTRODUCTION

"Seeing the Elephant" is an old American phrase that refers to gaining experience in the world at a significant cost. It's also associated with the military as seeing combat.[1] At almost 49 years old, I thought I'd "Seen the Elephant" in my life, but as I opened my eyes to find a police officer at the foot of the bed, I instantly knew I had been mistaken.

The officer began asking me questions; confusion overcame me, and I struggled to answer. I quickly learned I had experienced a major seizure and my wife, Catherine, had rendered first aid and called 911. In my typical workaholic ways, I insisted on walking downstairs, cell phone in hand while I walked to the ambulance. The emergency room doctors stated Catherine's training years before in seizure first aid resulted in her near-perfect response upon waking to my seizure at 5:00 a.m. on March 1, 2018. Within two hours, they transported me to a hospital with neurosurgery specialists. Seven days later, a brain tumor the size of a small apple, that had been growing for 15 years or more on my optic nerve, was removed from my frontal lobe.

Pre-surgery, the doctor advised I would lose my sense of taste and smell and possibly ... my sight. Worse still, they informed me I might not remember my wife (while still in our first year of marriage). Despite my wish to just deal with circumstances, Catherine rightly insisted on calling my adult sons who traveled across the country to see me. Work colleagues wished me well, but they have since admitted they thought, at best, I'd become a "vegetable" and might not survive. Catherine's daddy and children came to be with her both to support me but also, thinking I wouldn't survive, to support her. My dad, sister, and her family were there, steadfast as always but worried. Although fearful, I focused on getting through the operation and started on recovery. I had faith all would be well.

I had come to believe I was made of strong material and essentially unbreakable. As an adult, I'd survived being lit on fire, beaten with brass knuckles and held at knifepoint by four thugs, caught in an industrial paper cutter, threatened with a loaded gun by an irate man, "tackled" a pick-up truck, and nearly taken out by a bout of antibiotic-resistant pneumonia in the ICU. In fact, in 2004 in the Harrisonburg ICU, I was so sick they wanted to medevac me to a better hospital but were convinced I would die in transit. So, all they could do was keep me there and see if I would improve. Despite the prognosis, I walked out of the hospital four days later and continued my travel to my new job in New Jersey. I held strong to the belief that if I was knocked down, I got back up.

That trait runs strong in my family, and I was good at overcoming the odds. However, I've come to realize that despite my unbreakable self-image, the biggest factor was a huge number of family and friends were all praying and hoping for the best.

I awoke after the operation, and to everyone's surprise, I was alert, impatient, and wanting to start recovery. My vision, hearing, taste, and hand-eye coordination were dramatically improved. That was only the beginning. My speed of thought improved, and I didn't need rehabilitation, radiation, or chemotherapy. The nerve damage I thought I had on the right side of my face (from the brass knuckle incident years before) was eradicated instantly. I walked out of the hospital six days later. They wanted to use me as a case study, all the while admitting they didn't understand the result. I played guitar again within five minutes of getting home, and I only used four painkillers at home because I only felt pain for a short amount of time. Also, I am now nearly completely ambidextrous.

My dad, a 40-year medical professional, admitted post-surgery he had seen the MRI and talked with the neurosurgeon, and there was essentially zero chance I could have been functioning with a tumor of that size. However, clearly, I had been working 12-hour days, six to seven days a week for years, traveling the world and showing almost no symptoms prior to the seizure. Not even a headache! I have since found some scientific studies which say a long-term pianist's brain "rewires" itself in a way that made me function before and after surgery. They fact I have played piano 43 years in itself produced a miracle, to which I have given thanks to my mom, a retired music teacher.

How can I explain I saw my grandmother and great-aunt, who passed away several years ago, visit me post-surgery and tell me I would be all right? What was that about? I called my aunt in Maine and told her I hadn't believed her when she said her grandfather visited her when he passed away in 1985. I confessed that whatever the reason, I now had complete faith it had occurred.

I now steadfastly believe it was the prayers of a large number of friends and family that made the difference. How was I so blessed to have a wife trained in seizure response? How did I come to live only five minutes from a hospital? I have learned it was *ego* that made me think I was unbreakable. Yes, I had been blessed with a high pain-tolerance and excellent healing abilities. Yes, I had faith all would be well. Yes, I fought back from bad circumstances. However, none of these are *my* accomplishments. I have now truly "Seen the Elephant" in that I have experienced my form of combat and life experience. I have "Seen the Elephant" and contradictorily emerged both humbled and stronger than before. Conquering these obstacles didn't happen alone. It was through the blessings of God and the prayers and faith of family and friends. That was in fact the key to all of my prior victories, not my own capabilities. It is now up to me to make the most of the opportunity granted to me to share this with others and to take advantage of every day.

Experiencing a long and varied career and seeing a lot of the world has been a benefit to me. In fact, my average of times between moves is still less than three years, and I've never lived in the same place twice. I was recently asked about how many cities I had worked in. In my professional career, I worked in 16 countries and 98 cities, and I lived in 10 different cities. I've worked for both small mom and pop operations to Fortune 500 companies. This all leads to a lot of mileage from the perspective of Indiana Jones. In other words, I gained a fair amount of experience and adventures I wouldn't

"Seeing the Elephant"—An Introduction

necessarily have received living in only one place and working for only a few companies.

A sampling of license plates from Robert's vehicles through the years.

 This book turns these unique adventures into something of a playbook for people facing challenging situations in business. The names have been changed to protect the guilty (and the innocent).
 Music has always helped me keep sane in an insane business world, so I've also used different songs to tie the different chapters together. As a starting point, you can say, as the Eagles sing in The Long Run, I'm "Kinda bent, but we ain't broken" at this point in my career. I'm still standing and moving forward, even though I have gained some bruises and scrapes along the way. Sharing some tales of my adventures, as well as family history tales, and approaches developed along the way should help you in your career.

LEADERSHIP, NOT MANAGEMENT

"You need to be in the Dallas office at 9 a.m. tomorrow," the voice on the phone from headquarters said. *Ugh. Well, I guess telling off my boss just got me fired.* At least that was what I thought. It had been a hard nine months working with my boss, Anthony. He officed in Dallas and came down to Austin once or twice a month to visit. He had odd habits, such as requiring us to put small, round mirrors on our phones to remind us to smile when we answered calls. He was erratic, irritable, but definitely enthusiastic. It took me a while to figure out what was going on. When I did, it was all due to a shared bathroom with a key.

He would arrive in the morning full of enthusiasm and did this weird sniffing thing with his nose, and he moved at about 100 miles per hour. I struggled to keep up with him despite having multiple cups of coffee. This would last about an hour, then he would slow down dramatically. About then, he would get the bathroom key, be gone for five minutes, then show up at 100 miles per hour again. On and on (and on). After a few months, I had my theory firmly in place.

Anthony also was prone to taking short-cuts that would help other locations and hurt mine. The final example was shifting inventory to my location that I couldn't use. In this way, the stronger locations looked even better, and my location would take a loss. That was the straw that broke this camel's back. On our call, I told him in very clear language that this was unacceptable and out of control. I believe I even went so far as to threaten to report him to his boss.

Here I was, now having spoken my mind, and not five minutes later, I was summoned to his office in Dallas.

When I arrived in Dallas, he was nowhere to be found, but all of the other managers had gathered. Anthony had been fired, and we were put under a new leader. Instantaneously, the incident with me speaking my mind was erased, and I got a new start. That is, until I had to clean out the company rented apartment he used in Austin, which was covered with this mysterious white powder all over the coffee table and the small mirrors we used on the office phones.

DON'T FOCUS ON THE "GREEN GRASS OF KENTUCKY"

There was a popular song recorded by numerous artists titled "I've Been Everywhere." They even recorded different versions for different regions of the world like the UK, New Zealand, and Australia. The North American version called out over 90 locations:[2]

Phew, makes me tired thinking of all that travel, even though I have been to 42 of the locations! The point of the song is that the singer is joyful about the places he's seen. He is acknowledging that he's seen them but enjoying where he is at the moment. A strong leader in business also focuses on the future, not the past. Remember that there is no such thing as standing still in business. Rather, every day, your business is either getting stronger or weaker. As a leader, you must use your influence to make it stronger.

The Alps in Switzerland

I came from a generation of movers. In fact, I've never lived in the same location twice, and I averaged moving every two to three years. My parents taught me early on to "keep looking forward." Every move was a new adventure and something to be looked forward to being a part of. This did not take away from where we had been but kept us from feeling victimized because we were forced to move to new places. Therefore, I was shocked standing with a view high in the Alps in Switzerland, seeing row upon row of snow-covered mountains as far as the eye could see when the gentleman standing next to us told his wife, "Yup, these are nice but not nearly as nice as the green grass in Kentucky."

I was at a loss for words, even at seven years old. Was he not seeing the same view as I was? The reality was, we were both seeing the same view but with different lenses. Rather than enjoying where he was at the moment and realizing he would go home to Kentucky soon; he was looking backward while I was looking forward and enjoying the moment. The truth is, I have never been back to Switzerland since that time but enjoy the view and memory still without it being corrupted by other images. I've used that encounter in Switzerland to look forward and lead in a number of organizations.

You Snuck on My Blindside While I Was Shuckin' These Peas!

As teenagers, we liked living in Colorado, but we knew we would have to leave sometime because of my dad's job. It happened when he was offered a flight surgeon's position (which fulfilled his dream of being a pilot). It was a good opportunity. However, southern Alabama was a long way from Colorado and was almost like getting in a time machine to the past. Well, we were on track to make it to Ozark—what would become my next hometown—by our deadline and pulled up to a gas station along the road. We rounded a corner and frightened a local lady sitting outside who exclaimed, "You snuck up on my blindside while I was shuckin' these peas!" That was the exact moment we knew we were in for a new adventure in the South.

I definitely didn't fit in with long hair and black rock and roll T-shirts. In fact, things didn't get better until I cut my hair. However, I only cut it because it was too hot to work in an un-airconditioned bike shop. Surprisingly, I began to make more friends. Despite the odds, some of my best friends are from those two years, and I even returned to the state to go back to school over ten years later. By cutting my hair, I was unintentionally leaning forward into my new environment rather than looking backward to Colorado.

My First Real Job!

I had the privilege of joining a company still run by its founder. While I was on assignment in another state, he sold the company after running it for over 20 years. We became professionalized, and the culture rapidly changed. Was it all for good? Absolutely not. In fact, we experienced layoff after layoff and new leadership in multiple positions. However, being raised the way I was, I was promoted four times in the following four years. How did that occur? Other than being in the right place at the right time, I believe it was due to constantly being willing to try new things and learn new skills. I gained a reputation of being a leader able to adjust quickly, solve problems, and adapt. This served me well then and has served me well in several other companies through the years.

Train Yourself to Look Forward

It is often stated that people will hold three or more careers doing completely different things in their lifetimes and often at different companies. You will likely "be everywhere," as the song states, before your career is finished. Here are some steps and ideas to help you lead in rapidly changing situations:

1. Make a list of the good things you know about your current situation. Keep this list with you and add to it regularly.
2. Keep your eyes open for new possibilities in your situation.
3. Train yourself—read or take a course in the areas of new possibilities.
4. Don't wait to be perfect to raise your hand to help out in a new area. While others are focused on what they have lost, you can be the one helping out moving your organization forward.
5. Adapt as needed. The single act of cutting my hair, although unplanned, helped me with new opportunities in Alabama. I was the same person with shorter hair, but it helped me. Be willing to change.

IF YOU LEAVE LATE, IT JUST GETS LATER AND LATER

Johnny Cash had a hit in the 1970s with a song titled "One Piece at a Time." Not that I am advocating stealing from a car manufacturer, but when he realized he wanted a car but couldn't afford it, he began sneaking out pieces over the course of 25 years. Despite the fact that he had an odd-looking car whose "title weighed 60 pounds," he did not wait around for something to happen.[3] Rather, he developed a plan, took action, and adjusted course where needed to reach his objective. You should plan and develop a roadmap, but more importantly, you shouldn't wait for perfection. Take action and encourage action every day.

Consensus Management—Delays

I talked to a recent client, and it was clear in early February 2019 they needed our assistance with the implementation of a new technology. Our focus wasn't on the technology but rather on developing the processes to go along with that technology. The project was moving full-speed ahead with the first "go-live" of the technology scheduled for August. That was good news, as we could get started on the work rapidly.

However, the organization focused heavily on consensus management rather than operating in a command-and-control fashion. They simply refused to order anyone else, either their direct teams or colleagues, to do something. It took until late July, three weeks before go-live, for us to be brought in to help. For those of you keeping score at home, I made over 100 contacts (phone calls, face-to-face meetings, and emails) between February and July to get everyone in agreement.

They had a plan, or roadmap, so the project turned out well, but it meant we played a lot of catch up in August and September to get problems solved and the right new processes in place. They left late, and it just got later and later! We were in conversation with the client for some new work, and right at the point of getting consensus, a new individual interjected, and the work had been delayed. This delay cost the client valuable savings that could have been used to achieve their core mission. Meanwhile, they laid off staff, an action that could have been avoided if they had acted more rapidly.

Squirrels Chasing Shiny Objects

Have you ever seen squirrels, or other critters, get distracted by the shiny object and forget what they were doing? I saw two blue jays fighting over peanuts in the back yard. They were so focused on fighting each other that they let other birds steal their peanuts. After the fight, one of them sat there and looked around befuddled, probably thinking, *Who stole my peanuts?* They acted but the forgot the plan was to get the peanuts.

I've seen this happen many times in business. One of the earliest companies I worked at—still run at the time by the founding entrepreneur—was one of those. He constantly came up with new ideas. Some of them were great, and some were not so great. However, he had the habit of always focusing on the new thoughts. We would be pursuing one of his ideas that had merit, and after working on it for months, he would get bored with the concept and drop it before we reached the outcome. Rather than achieve new benefits, we were left with wasted effort, resources, and money for no benefit.

Another business founder was focused on having a physical operation in every geography *before* building the business locally. Why was this? It got to the point that the only rationale was that it was based on ego. It felt better to him to be able to say we were in all of these exotic locations, rather than travel to the locations, win some profitable work, and then build the physical locations. To give you an extreme example, they had a location in Asia for almost a year before any work was generated from the location.

Ronnie the Entrepreneur

I'll admit I really needed a job and was willing to settle for almost anything. The right thing had been done by quitting my college job. I needed to focus on my education. However, I still needed money to pay the bills and was tired of walking all over town going door to door asking for work. I was also tired of eating frozen ham—one slice a day—to stretch the food budget. Maybe I was in some sort of delusional ham haze when I talked to Ronnie.

Ronnie had recently bought the little 1940s diner across the road from the university I attended. He offered me the position of assistant manager, which I took. It wasn't a horrible job, despite the instance when the stove exploded and lit me on fire, but it rapidly worsened over several months.

It seemed Ronnie was born with what some would call the entrepreneur's spirit. He quickly took over a dance club called the Blue Hen on the other side of town. Then, he took on more space next to the diner and opened an arcade. I thought this might work as they all sort of tied together in the food/entertainment world. Next, he hired a guitarist who claimed to have played with Elvis to perform at the diner. Privately, I doubted this as I wondered what one of Elvis's guitarists was doing working at a diner in central Texas in 1989.

The next branching out was opening a laundromat behind the diner (in the same building) with the rationale that students could do their clothes while eating and studying in the diner. It took an even weirder turn when he opened a car wash behind the building. All of this happened in about four months' time. It could have looked like an entrepreneurial success story except that the core business was floundering, and he never had enough money. He couldn't even fully meet payroll every week. It reached its low point when I found myself racing my '76 VW Bug down Highway 29 against co-workers to see who could get to the bank first. The first one to the bank would win by their check being cashed. The losers would not get paid and have to deal with no money for their work. That was the end of the line for me. I resigned, focused on college finals for the semester, and moved into a new job in a couple of weeks. Things weren't finished with Ronnie, however, as he failed to issue tax documents at the end of the year, and I had to track him down so I could file my taxes. Ronnie was so focused on the next opportunity he didn't focus on making sure his business functioned properly. This quickly left him out of money and out of business.

A Lot of Shoes at Christmas

Do you know what your sales record or profit record is for your organization? Do you track these things on an ongoing basis? Would anyone know if you broke a record? I learned the importance of these things by working for my grandfather at his shoe store during the summertime and holidays.

We were back in town for Christmas, and we were down to only myself and my grandfather in the store on the last day we were open before Christmas. He'd had some tough times with competition lately. The town was known as the hometown of Richard Petty, the NASCAR champion. Traditionally, both Richard and his wife, Lynda, had bought shoes from us. Even almost 30 years after the store closed, I heard that when he was complimented on a pair of boots, he stated that he bought them at Hough's Shoes. However, this year, Kyle, their son, had, in addition to racing, opened a boot barn on the highway that took a fair bit of our business.

Robert's grandparents at their shoe store in North Carolina

My grandfather was always a numbers guy. And on this day, he recognized we were on track to possibly beat the best day of sales ever. This would be a significant sign that things were improving for the store. From that point on, we tracked every sale and used the opportunity to offer special pricing or combination sales to offer the customers a better value, and we would sell more.

At the end of the day, I still remember running the close-out routine on the cash register and calculating our daily sales. We had beat the record by a few dollars by staying open later in the evening. I learned an important lesson, not only about having measures for your business but also about being open with your team about the records and celebrating records being broken. On a side note, my grandfather shared advice in a newspaper article for his 50th Wedding Anniversary that talked openly about how finances were the key to a successful marriage[4].

Why That Mountain? What Should We Pack?

We were forming new teams after the big merger, myself from Compaq Computer and Alejandro from HP. Alejandro and I were talking, and he pointed out the differences in cultures between the two companies. He said, "You Compaq folks get told to go climb that mountain, and you just take off climbing! It might be the wrong mountain, you might get lost, you often change mountains mid-climb, but you are always moving."

I found it hard to argue with that. It was so ingrained in the Compaq company culture that had "recently" started in 1982 in a pie shop as opposed to HP, a company founded in the 1930s. He then went on and said, "If we HP folks are told to climb a mountain, we form a committee and begin debating. We ask questions, like why that mountain, what should we pack, who should go first? Should we go to that other mountain instead?" This certainly fit with the experience I had with HP folks. He then added, "But the funny thing is, by the time we've figured out what to do, you've reached the right mountain and achieved the goal."

He was right but the bigger point is that we needed to blend the cultures. We needed a bit more planning and getting the right mountain first, then taking rapid action would make us better together than either was independently. This was completely different than too much planning with no action while it was just getting later and later.

Rapidly Get on "The Road"

Just as Johnny Cash sang about adapting to fitting the different pieces of the car together that didn't fit, you need to act and then adjust. A few ideas for this are

1. Develop your plan but don't wait for it to be perfect. This applies to whether it's for a project or a longer-term objective. *See the appendix for a project plan example.*
2. Hold your ego in check. Ensure there are good business objectives for your plan—and it isn't just based on your ego.
3. Put measurements in the plan with specific numbers, dates, and accomplishments.
4. Act every day, moving yourself forward.
5. Look at your measurements frequently and adjust course as you learn more.
6. Repeat and set new objectives as you progress.

Always remember, "If you leave late, it just gets later and later," so get on the road and move forward!

YOU GET WHAT YOU NEED

The Rolling Stones sang, "You can't always get what you want" meaning it's more likely you get what you need instead.[5]

How does this apply in business? Asking for what you want can get you what you need. Don't being afraid to stretch yourself and push the limits. Even if you don't get what you want, you often end up in a better place. Negotiating is easier when you understand what you want and what you truly need.

I Can't Live on What I'm Worth

Whenever I'm negotiating with a new client or for a new job, I remind myself of a boss I had who did an excellent job of negotiating for his salary in a new role with a new company. On top of that, he did it with a sense of humor and humility.

After a long day of interviewing, my (soon to be) boss had dinner with the CEO of the company. After small talk and debriefing on the day's conversations, the CEO turned to him and said, "Larry, I'm really thinking you are the right fit for the CFO job, and I'd like to offer you the job." Larry replied that he was appreciative and very interested. The CEO then said, "Now, the important thing is, I want to make sure we pay you what you are worth."

My boss replied, "Oh no, I can't afford to live on what I'm worth. I'm going to need a lot more than that!" The immediate result, the CEO laughed aloud and said, "Well then, what do you want?" Although the CFO didn't receive his want, he achieved more pay than he would have, got his need met, and did it with a sense of humor.

Pay Me to Drive It Off the Lot

Last year, I found myself unexpectedly needing a second car. It needed to be a reliable used car at a low price. Beyond the basics of finding a dealer I could trust; I was challenged to make sure I got my point across and didn't end up paying more than I wanted due to limited cash. I decided to use the same approach as my boss' sense of humor. When asked what I wanted to pay for the car, typically one of the early questions, my response was "I'd like you to offer to pay me to drive one of your cars off the lot. That would free up space for you to sell more cars in the future." I knew the chances were zero for achieving that want, but that was ok with me. One hundred percent of the time, they responded with laughter. Better still, they understood immediately that I wanted a reliable car, but nothing extra, at a reasonable price. In fact, the dealer I bought from thought of a former buyer he was trying to help sell her car. He connected me and made the deal at a very reasonable price. He also acted very quickly. I got the car I needed at a price better than my budget.

Get What You Need

Remember, as the song said, "You can't always get what you want." However, there are a number of ways to negotiate more effectively to get what you need. These include

1. Be true to yourself. Don't try to use a sense of humor if you aren't confident in your ability. If candor works better, then follow that path.
2. Have a plan going in of what you want and what you will settle for. In my case with the used car, I needed to pay $5,000 maximum for a reliable used car—and wanted it for free. Therefore, when I was offered the right car for $3,400, it was easy to make a quick decision.
3. Be reasonable. It will be nice if you get you want, but it is most important that you get what you need in the situation. Be careful not to confuse the two!

DON'T BLINDFOLD YOUR BOSS

Cheap Trick rose to fame after several years as a band with their song "I Want You to Want Me" from the album *Live at Budokan*, which focuses on being wanted, needed, and loved.[6]

Sometimes as an employee or as a consultant, you feel the same way. You want to be needed and loved. However, sometimes it goes very differently, and you may be the cause.

Transparency Is a Frightening Thing

As we start a project involving multiple departments, our practice is to hold a kick-off meeting with key stakeholders and other project team members. We were in our meeting with the human resources department, and the head of HR, Beth, was sitting right next to me in our big circle. Our first task was to introduce ourselves and what we wanted in the project. I thought it would be great to start with myself, go to my right, then have the 15 other people introduce themselves, closing with the Head of HR. That would let Beth's team members speak first—and she could sum it all up. What could go wrong?

The conversations were good, and soon we reached Beth. She said briefly, "I'm Beth. I'm the Head of HR. I don't believe in this project and would like the earth to open up and swallow you consultants whole."

Ok, so I paraphrased a bit there, but that was clearly the message. She was near retirement, and she didn't want anything to do with the project. Unsurprisingly, her department fell in line with her views, and my team had the greatest difficulty with this group in meeting our objectives. We didn't get them to love, want, or need us. They just wanted us gone. I made the choice not to take the matter to a higher level in the organization as I was concerned that escalation would only make matters worse. We did meet the objectives, but it required far more work than would have been needed had they cooperated. Additionally, with escalation and better cooperation, we could have offered more savings opportunities to the whole organization but were unable to do so.

The Russians Are Going to Invade!

"We already know we want to move operations to Poland. There's no reason to prepare an analysis of potential locations." Well, that sounded like great news from the client. However, in my experience, someone always asks, even if much later, about the rationale for major project decisions. I therefore informed them we would do a light analysis, called a "Location Analysis" and have it prepared, just in case to support the decision. In other words, I politely told the client, "No, you are going to have to trust me that we need to do this."

The bottom line was that Poland was the right location given their existing operations in Poland (as the fourth largest country in sales in Europe) and the mix of talent and costs. We continued with our migration and transformation efforts across the next nine months. The site was about ¾ finished when we got the ominous phone call. The head of real estate in the U.S. had stopped work on the location. His rationale being, "The Russians are going to invade Poland any day now and we shouldn't locate there.". The location analysis that we had prepared came in handy. By the way, the head of real estate was previously in the U.S. government and kept referring to sources of information which he couldn't disclose. His position was weakened through the location analysis work. However, he still didn't want to be wrong. To break the impasse, I had to ask him to disclose his sources so we could evaluate his information. He refused to give us the information, further weakening his point. Finally, I was left with one more tool to use. I informed the client's team, "You realize that if the Russian's invade Poland, you have much bigger issues than where your accounting team is located, right? Like World War III and the loss of one of your biggest revenue sources in Europe?" When put in that perspective, they allowed the tools to be picked up, and the location finished. Even with the work we had done, the project was still delayed by six weeks. The situation could have been better managed by identifying and working with *all* of the stakeholders earlier in the process.

The Project Manager Was Arrested

Despite getting off to a bumpy start on our initial six-week project, things smoothed out after we overcame a significant obstacle, and it even appeared it would lead to more potential down the road. The project leader, Logan, who had won the project, was supposed to travel to the U.S. and be onsite and meet us at the client's office. At the last minute, I got the call that Logan hadn't been able to leave his home country.

Naturally, I asked what happened. "He was pulled off the plane by the federal authorities and arrested".

Well, that was unexpected. "Is he guilty?"

"No, he assures me it's just a misunderstanding. Tell the client that you are acting project leader, and he will be there in a few days."

So, my first role leading a project as a consultant was this one. I was glad it was getting off to a smooth start! We needed clients to love our work, and this was the opposite of the appropriate way to start a project.

I arrived, gave them the brief explanation, and we moved forward. It was no big deal other than the five of us being crammed into one tiny office on the second floor. I felt like we were being kept hidden. Fast forward to week three. My boss arrived with the news that Logan had been terminated due to the seriousness of the charges. He was trying to figure out what to say to the client. I came up with the only workable answer. After all, telling the client their main contact had been arrested for embezzling funds from his son's sports team was taking the full truth a step too far.

"Tell them, 'Logan has found himself dealing with a personal matter and won't be able to join the project.'"

"Well, what if they ask what it is?"

"Well, then, the response is 'it's a personal matter for him—I'm sure you understand I can't disclose it.'"

He followed the script, and the client didn't give it another thought. We were producing good results, and that was all they cared about. They were loving the work so far; despite the unseen obstacles we had faced.

At the end of the project, we produced a solid report with a roadmap to more work they could perform to save money and improve efficiency. Imagine our surprise when we didn't get the work.

Why not? Because the key project lead, the chief accounting officer, hadn't told his boss he had brought in consultants (remember being hidden in that cramped office?) nor told him about the project itself. He sprung it on the CFO in a group staff meeting. That went over like a lead balloon, and the CFO began giving orders to take other actions and involve other people. At this point, it's been over six years, and the work we recommended still hasn't commenced.

Removing the Blindfold

How do you remove the blindfold and avoid these problems with stakeholders? How do you get them to love, need, and want you in the workplace? A few ways include

1. Identify Your Key Stakeholders. In hindsight, how did I miss asking the question about the CFO's view of the project? I assumed, and it cost our client the opportunity to improve. *See the appendix for a sample Project Stakeholder Chart and Weekly Project Update Example.*
2. Talk with the Key Stakeholders regularly. Develop a communication mechanism to make sure they understand what is happening. Listen to their feedback and act upon it.
3. Escalate if necessary. In the case of the head of HR in my earlier example, I could have escalated the issues more aggressively with hopes of getting more cooperation. By not doing so, it cost my client

significant improvement opportunities. Thankfully, we overachieved in other areas, but we could have seen more improvements with better escalation.

DON'T BELIEVE YOUR OWN PRESS CLIPPINGS

Jackson Browne performed a song live in the 1970s called "The Load Out," paying tribute to both the roadies who loaded and unloaded his equipment, as well as the fans who came to his concerts. The song speaks to the power of his fans and supporters.[7]

This is not the perspective of a superstar. Rather, this is someone who realizes without his fans, he doesn't have a career or get to fulfill his dreams. This is also the same person who Glenn Frey of the Eagles said he heard practicing the same music over and over until he had it figured out. He realized nothing came easy, and it always required work.[8]

How does this tie to not believing your own press clippings? It has to do with maintaining humility with your team and customers. Both your team and your customers are the reason you can stay in business and achieve your dreams. You must build and keep engaging with them to maintain success. However, it's easy to lose perspective of this. I've gathered a few examples of how this can happen and tips for avoiding these types of situations.

The Manager Walk

The key is to get there quickly—but not look like you are in a panic. As a leader, or manager, your job often turns into putting out fires. In my case, sometimes this has been literally putting out fires. However, nothing freaks out both your team and your customers more quickly than seeing a manager running from place to place. Without a doubt, you feel like running to solve a problem. However, this causes more worry and disruption. People feel like everything is out of control, and panic frequently ensues. As the manager, you don't want to walk into the trap of feeling you are the savior of the operation—or in other words, making everything about you.

I learned a technique I call "The Manager Walk." You walk very quickly toward the crisis of the moment. There is no running, but it is almost as fast. However, instead of instilling panic in your team and customers, it looks like you are in charge. You walk with authority.

Do you really have a clue what you are doing? Sometimes you do not! However, by responding with apparent calm, situations are quickly diffused. Running around a corner and skidding to a stop in front of an irate customers *does not help* solve problems.

Last year, a customer made me aware of a situation he faced in his business. He ran a dessert shop in town and put 50s rock and roll over his Bluetooth speakers in his business. While he was in the back in the shop, he noticed sounds that were definitely not rock and roll coming from his speakers. Mothers were covering their children's ears while rushing them out the door. He came to the front of the shop and discovered pornography audio was being broadcast over his speakers. On top of that, he heard the guy in the rented room upstairs laughing! To his credit, he calmly used his manager walk up the stairs and knocked on the guy's door. He asked the guy to come outside—and to stop hijacking his Bluetooth speakers. Of course, the guy refused, but the business owner didn't make it worse by acting in a panic. He also learned a lesson in password protecting his computer systems!

I Am an Officer's Wife!

My great-grandmother, Henrietta, immigrated from Germany to the United States as a teenager. She came from humble origins, as did my great-grandfather, Wilbur. He decided he didn't like the prospect of carrying on the tradition of being a farmer in Maine, lied about his age, and joined the Army at 15 years old. Through a long career, he advanced to being promoted from a private to a captain and served for years in Panama and the Philippines. Life as a U.S. Army officer's wife in the Philippines in the 1920s was along the lines of being royalty. You had the best of the area, including servants to cook and clean for you, the best houses, and participation in events with the other officers (and their wives), like General MacArthur. After living this life for well over ten years, when Wilbur retired, he became the chief of police for the State of Maine, and the luxury life continued. After all, he was working directly for the governor of the state. She absolutely lost touch with humility during these times. It all came crashing down, however, and he died in 1944 from a disease he caught in the Philippines.

However, after 25 years of living in the same manner, Henrietta continued to live as if she was still an officer's wife. In many ways, her behavior was disconnected from her day-to-day circumstances. This wasn't the only area of disconnection. As a fairly recent German immigrant, she couldn't conceive of the changes the Nazis had brought during World War II. In fact, my grandmother had to step in and stop her from going to the press when she wanted to talk about my grandfather being a POW in German territory. This could have turned out very badly, as my grandfather was half-German, spoke German, and was doing his best to keep this a secret as he would be seen as a traitor to Germany. My grandmother (her daughter-in-law) continued watching over her financial (and personal) situations. This included forcing her to get an annulment when she remarried in the 1950s. This was because my great-grandmother hadn't realized her new husband had no money or income, and that by remarrying, she would be giving up the Spanish-American War pension. She was a wonderful person, doting on my father and wanting well for all, but was not grounded in reality. She lived almost 40 years after my great-grandfather passed away but rarely shook the entitled behavior, even when her treasured possessions gathered from world travel had to be sold for her continued care. She had lost humility, as many of us can, and believed her own press clippings. This caused her harm in the long run, just as it can each of us in both our lives and careers.

Long Live the King!

My boss of several years left our organization for a promotion and new role as a Divisional CFO in another state. Although I wouldn't have described him as humble while working for him, he was definitely approachable and had a strong character. After much discussion and being given the option internally of spending another five to seven years in the same role before a promotion, I took him up on his offer for a new opportunity with a new organization. It sounded like a new adventure and the opportunity to keep the rust from building up on my skills. It was certainly that but much more. I saw first-hand how someone's behavior can change in a new environment and turn from humility to entitlement.

In hindsight, I can see my boss always knew how to manage up, but this behavior became his fundamental approach in his new role. In fact, it appeared he never told his new manager, the division CEO, the word "no" or presented him with the risks of potential decisions. This is the same CEO who, when I was giving a presentation to him, was so disengaged he sat there staring out the window while chewing his Styrofoam cup to bits and spitting the pieces out on the table. Not exactly a warm and fuzzy leader.

For example, the company saw a potentially good acquisition; however, it was overpriced by three to four times. Our team knew we needed to negotiate the price down for it to be successful. However, our CEO was adamant he wanted to buy it without negotiation

Our CFO was our last line of defense, but he did not offer his opinion to the CEO, and the company was acquired at their asking price. This was an Internet-based company, and as we dealt with the assimilation of the business, it became apparent there were issues.

We first noticed the coming problems when we started gathering financial information. They were not on our financial system yet, but rather than sending the information via email in files, they were printing and faxing the information to us. This was in the 2000s and well past the days of using the fax machine on a daily basis. Fast-forward a few months, and we realized their response to search requests on their revenue-generating services were taking one to two minutes, rather than five to ten seconds.

No one was willing to wait for search results taking that long. Potential customers moved on to a competitor's website. As a result, the revenue plummeted. We began an intense effort to rebuild the technology with brand new software, but this effort took several months. By that time, it was the end of the fiscal year, and we had to write down the value of the acquisition. What was the value? That was 25 percent of the acquisition price and almost exactly what was predicted nine months earlier. It actually got worse, as it caused the entire company to miss annual predictions and resulted in the company being broken up into multiple parts, causing massive work and layoffs to staff.

Why did this happen? While the CEO was responsible, it also appears the big promotion resulted in the CFO believing his own press clippings, losing his humility, and not being willing to be the objective, rational CFO. The truth is, this can happen to all of us if we are not careful.

Being Humble as a Leader

How do you demonstrate humility to your people and customers in the way that Jackson Browne stated in "The Load Out?" Here are a few simple steps to help you:

1. Surround yourself with people who are real. These folks should tell you the truth.
2. Have a mentor. Everyone, no matter how accomplished, can use advice and someone to discuss issues with on an ongoing basis.
3. Listen to these people. No one is perfect, and there is always room for improvement.

4. Build a team of rivals. President Lincoln surrounded himself with people with more talents and abilities than he had. Have the confidence to do the same.[9]

It isn't easy as you advance in leadership roles but keep these ideas in mind to stay humble while developing as a leader.

HR TIPS THAT HR MIGHT NOT APPROVE OF

A colleague used to refer to the effects of working at one company as "self-esteem leakage." What in the world was that? His theory wasn't that different from saying one straw breaks the camel's back. It isn't actually one straw—it's the culmination of a whole lot of straws over time. His viewpoint was that on a day-to-day basis, dealing with management in the workplace was resulting in "self-esteem leakage." He felt that that being corrected, managed, mis-managed, mis-directed, and changing direction was hurtful to employees. Any single act wasn't that bad. Employee management is always challenging, particularly when management changes direction. However, without strong change management activities, if this happens every day for years, slowly, your self-esteem leaks, much like a slow leak from a tire on your car. Yes, you can put more air in, but it just leaks out. You aren't fixing the leak or getting a new tire.

What can you do about this? As a leader, think about whether you are causing these leaks. Are you building the person up, or are you only having conversations about what they are doing wrong? Are you refilling the tire? Are you helping them build new skills? The building of these new skills is the equivalent of getting a new tire.

SOMETIMES IT'S IHOP TIME!

Billy Joel had a song called "Say Goodbye to Hollywood." A key section of the song speaks to people flowing in and out of your life.[10] Essentially, he says almost nothing is permanent. This is critical to remember in business and in life. It is especially important to decide when to move on and how to deal with it if you reach what I refer to as "iHop Time."

But She Isn't a Witch!

In the 1670s in Hampton, New Hampshire, my great-great (ok, I've lost track of how many *greats* she was) grandmother, Isabella, became caught up in the witchcraft hysteria sweeping the area. She and her husband, Philip, were part of a group of 20 families who founded the town. Isabella was minding her business and raising eight children between 18 months old and 18 years old. As I understand it, a neighbor's cow didn't give milk, and a local woman was accused of witchcraft. However, if she gave up her fellow witches, her life would be spared. Being too good an offer to pass up when faced with death, she accused Isabella of witchcraft. Isabella was arrested and held in jail for nine months. Eventually, the hysteria subsided a bit and Philip, with borrowed money, paid the fines to get her out of jail. However, both of them were convinced their time in Hampton was done. They didn't argue or fight; they simply picked up and moved outside of the town to live with the Native Americans. Today, their old (new) homestead is inside the town boundaries, and they have been recognized as co-founders of the town. As a side-note, the ringleader of the witches was also absolved of guilt in the early 1900s.[11] I can't imagine how hard it would have been to leave a place you've helped found, but I've learned a lot of lessons in business that taught me when it was time to move on.

2 + 2 Doesn't Equal 5

I've lost two jobs for refusing to falsify numbers. In both cases, I had short-term concerns (and second thoughts), but in the long-term, I have had zero regrets about my decisions. The first occurred in 1996 and the second in 2012.

1996: I suddenly found myself with a pregnant wife on bedrest and a two-year-old son, and I was also laid off. Somehow, a layoff of one feels very personal. Probably because it is very, very personal. How did this happen? The founder of the company had sold the company several years before, leaving the company in the hands of the new owners. The day before, I told my boss, "I found information on the annual survey has apparently, since the founder's departure, been falsified and could lead to U.S. Federal charges."

I did it without hesitation, not even thinking about the potential consequences other than doing the right thing. With the surprise layoff, I faced a choice between a limited few weeks of pay or a protracted legal battle. I signed the paperwork, and I committed to moving on and not saying another word to anyone in the organization.

On the very positive side, my second son was born several months later, my wife improved, and I spent considerable time bonding with my two-year-old. After several months of unemployment, I wished the job consequences were different, but I inherently felt I had done the right thing.

With no job and a lot of free time, I found myself with a fair amount of time to think. For years, I felt like a failure because I didn't "finish Scouts properly" by achieving the ultimate goal of earning the rank of Eagle Scout. In fact, I was a young Life Scout with most of the merit badges, membership in the "Order of the Arrow," and the required project planned. Rather, I let a move from Colorado to Alabama, high school, a part-time job, and a garage band form excuses to let the goal go. Now at 27, I couldn't support my growing family, but I had the opportunity to think about why my response was automatic and without hesitation. Let's look deeper at the Scout Law.

On my honor I will do my best ... to keep myself ... morally straight.

Hmmm. Perhaps I hadn't failed by moving on from Scouts. Perhaps I'd learned something far more important than earning a rank. Did this account for my instinctive reaction? I then looked at the Scout Law. Examine these excerpts:

A Scout is:

Trustworthy: Tell the truth and keep promises. People depend on you.

Brave: Face difficult situations even when you feel afraid. Do what you think is right despite what others might be doing or saying.[12]

Eleven-plus years after moving on from scouting, I wondered if I was still living the code. Isn't that the organization's ultimate goal? Which sticks with you further? I moved on to other opportunities. They included a mixture of failures and successes, along with moves from Texas to New Jersey and now Virginia. I'm proud to say that I have never compromised my core integrity. Have there been setbacks and conflicts? Absolutely. Would I do anything differently? That is an interesting question. I did, in fact, wonder from time to time about the cost of doing the right thing. Did I hurt my family just to save my skin from being involved in a crime, or was there some greater reason and impact?

Fast-forward to a company reunion with the founder 21-plus years after my departure. It was a fun event reuniting a number of us with the founder of the company. Toward the end of the night, a former co-worker approached me and stated (in front of the founder), "I want you to know I know what was going on in 1996 and how you refused to be part of it." He went on to say, "I have used your positive example with all of my teams over the last 20 years of how to stay true to your beliefs, despite the consequences". There, after 21 years, was my answer. My actions, despite their cost, had unknowingly been used positively for all of this time, cascading forward from person to person.

Internalizing the importance of the Scout Oath and Law had in fact made a difference and a positive, greater impact. I hope my four children—two of which are Eagle Scouts, one a former scout and an Army Special Forces Ranger, and one a former Girl Scout—learned that beyond the ranks and experiences, there are far more important lessons to take with them forward in life. Moving on can be exactly the right thing to do.

The Pinkerton Vanishing Act

A similar situation occurred to me when I was the vice-president of finance for Pinkerton Consulting and Investigations. I had been in the CFO role for 18 months, and we were growing rapidly through making a number of acquisitions. Preparing the financial analysis for the newest potential acquisition, I felt comfortable we would hit the required financial returns and turned this into the new president of the organization. He was formerly in finance for another division of the company and a known favorite of the North American CEO of the parent corporation. I was surprised when the next day, I came in and found he had increased the estimated profits and financial return in the model. I debated this with him as my name was still affixed to the analysis and disagreed. Additionally, this was unnecessary as the original document completely supported the acquisition and would set us up to look like we failed if we didn't hit these higher expectations. He didn't respond favorably to my response, and the same day, I found myself laid off from the company. Interestingly enough, I was part of a chain of exits as the new leader cleaned house and relocated the company headquarters closer to his home. In this case, I didn't look back and moved forward to consulting with organizations.

The Pleasure of the Governor

My great-grandfather served "at the pleasure of the Governor" as the Chief of Police for the State of Maine in the late 1930s.

1930s Maine State Policeman and his vehicle

After several years of success, a notable bank robbery occurred, and his team was tasked with investigating and bringing the culprits to justice. After a couple of weeks, he reported to the governor that his team was close to finding the culprits. The governor wanted him to stand down and stop the investigation. My great-grandfather refused as it went against his duties and integrity. The governor repeated his desire for the investigation to be stopped. Again, my great-grandfather refused. As he served "at the pleasure of the governor," he was then removed from his role. As the investigation continued, it came to light several members of the governor's cabinet were involved in the bank robbery. This led to their removal from office.[13] It was too late to return my great-grandfather to the same role, but his role in solving the crime and his integrity were respected. He was given a role leading another agency in the state government. He moved on when asked and didn't look back.

Congratulations on Your Demotion

It had been a really hard year for the organization. The rapid growth we had experienced tailed off, and our expansion into new business lines failed. As director of financial planning and analysis, I'd spent about six months trying to save the company and the executives. Although we survived, the leaders were all shown the door for failing to meet our annual forecast. I somehow stayed but was very closely associated with the previous regime.

I was in the middle of compiling our annual budgets for each of the locations when my new boss arrived in my office. In very fast fashion, he let me know I was being demoted and moved to reporting to one of my peers. He also let me know he thought I had grown about as much as possible with the organization. Then, he closed with saying how much he appreciated my support. The only thing I could really say was "thanks, Sam."

After sitting there for a minute, I then turned my attention back to the budgets. At home, I thought back over the conversation. How could a person halfway through a master's degree have grown about as much as possible? I was doing a good job and loyal to the company. My only conclusion was that it was time to go. The new boss had been clear: I was done in the organization. Over the next couple of weeks, I finished the budgets and looked forward to the Thanksgiving break. Over the break, I applied to two major companies. I quickly had interviews and was offered jobs in each. Choosing the one I felt was the best fit, I turned in my resignation before Christmas.

The look of shock was unbelievable. It was as if the new boss didn't expect me to take him seriously. I was starting in early January. "How will we get the work done without you in place?"

I'm still proud of my response. "I'll be more than happy to consult with you and assist during lunches and weekends." We negotiated the very good rate of $100 per hour. It was a bit of a shock to see them still needing consulting work six months later, but all of these years later, I'm still glad I "got the message" and moved on. I also still enjoy the bookshelves I purchased for myself with the consulting income!

The Captain Is Unconscious on His Desk

"The captain is unconscious on his desk," my father reported to the colonel in Panama. The captain was also my father's commanding officer.

The colonel replied, "Why is that, Chief?"

"Because I knocked him out," my father replied

As he replied, he was having visions of his 25-plus-year career rising from a private to a chief warrant officer 4 evaporate in a moment and ending in a military prison.

"Interesting. Tell me why you knocked him out" was the Colonel's response.

My father had been tasked with following a new organization system for medical response kits for soldiers in combat, and the captain refused to follow the new system. He was taking supplies from different kits and not following the process. My father explained numerous times to no avail. As a decorated veteran of the Vietnam War and serving in combat as a medic while a Green Beret, he fully understood the risk when troops were undersupplied. This was quite literally a life and death situation.

After several attempts and further escalation of the verbal altercations, my father threw a punch and knocked his commanding officer unconscious. Despite concerns for his future, he then went immediately upstairs and reported the incident to the colonel. To my father's surprise, the colonel responded, "We will take care of it, Chief" and promptly transferred the captain to a post in Alaska. My father's reputation for integrity and combat experience, in addition to essentially reporting himself for his actions, led to his career surviving the incident. Both the captain and my father moved on to new situations having learned some important lessons.

iHop Time

As promised, we are now getting to the phrase involving "iHop Time." I had been working for a client for several months, and truthfully, it wasn't smooth. Client demands and some staffing issues made it challenging. We had one consultant on our project walking around the client's office handing out copies of her resume, while another got on a conference call and admitted to the client, that he had done zero work for the last week. Imagine his surprise when I told him I couldn't pay him for the last week.

"Why not?" he asked.

"Because you told the client you had accomplished nothing in a week and have done no work," I replied. He sat there stunned.

I awoke in the hotel room in California to a phone call from my boss. The client was ending our engagement. It wasn't terribly surprising. I accepted it and prepared to go into the client's office and turn in my paperwork, badges, and hand over the work in process. "No, just check out of the hotel and leave" was my boss's reply. So, I did the only reasonable thing. I checked out and had a good breakfast at iHop, got on a plane, and left. In time, the phrase "sometimes it's just iHop time" worked its way into the company vernacular as a code for "every engagement will end—just move on".

Do you find yourself with "iHop time?" Is it time to move on? It's hard to say how you know as it might not be as obvious as it was in my case. However, I have a better understanding of my ancestor's reaction to the accusations of witchcraft. You have a choice to either stay and fight or move on. In cases where an argument is futile, it's better to set your sights on the future.

By the way, the California client came back a year later and needed help with worldwide customer service training, which we gladly provided. It wasn't personal; they just didn't need our help anymore in 2015. If I'd let it become personal, we would not have received the future work.

The Golden Canary and Rehydrated Peaches

My teammates and I loved Mr. West. He was the manager of the local Golden Corral and had not only hired me as assistant dishwasher but promoted me rapidly to dishwasher and then to working with customers on the line taking orders. I was tasked with refilling the salad bar. It wasn't glamorous work, but it was a solid job as a high school senior in a new town. Therefore, we were disappointed when we came into work one afternoon and found him gone and replaced with a new manager.

Mr. Henson was an entirely different story. He drove a blacked-out 1983 Buick Riviera and bragged about how many Golden Canary awards he'd received from the company. He liked to offer the young ladies rides in his Buick while we were supposed to be working and was, to put it bluntly, a slime bag.

The low point with Mr. Henson came due to an incident with the peaches on the salad bar. We had all been taught to not serve anything we wouldn't eat ourselves. So, when I saw a five-year-old hopped up on soda, running around, and sticking his dirty hands in the vat of sliced peaches, I dutifully went out, retrieved them, and dumped them in the trash. I then got a new batch out in a fresh container. However, soon, Mr. Henson came nosing around and asked, "What are all of these perfectly good peaches doing in the trash?"

Explaining the situation, he informed me, "You should have just rinsed them off with hot water." Deciding to play along, I asked how we would handle the absence of the syrup. "You would just rehydrate the peaches with syrup from the next can you opened."

My only response was "yes, sir, the next time that happens, I will do it that way" and promptly ignored him.

I'll have to admit I enjoyed it when my first anniversary came, and he neglected to give me my promised raise. When I asked him about it, he informed me that since I was leaving for college in six weeks, he wasn't giving me one. He looked a little shocked when I gave him my two weeks' notice and enjoyed a month off. Life was too short to put up with his nonsense any longer.

How Dare You Spend $150!

I was recovering from what I refer to as my "minor cosmetic surgery," aka having a brain tumor removed from my frontal lobe which had been growing there for 15 years or more. Everything went well, and I was quickly back to limited work. However, it was critical to follow the doctor's orders, including limiting my computer or TV screen time to two hours a day. Two weeks after surgery, I was given the task of doing some research for a previous client in the attempt to win them back. No problem, except I couldn't devote the computer time for the writing and research. So, I found a solution. A local college senior, who I had known for a couple of years, was about to graduate with a degree in business, and it was the right solution. We negotiated a $15 an hour rate for ten hours of research. He did great work, and I spent my limited screen time polishing his work and aligning it to the client's needs. I paid him the $150 and turned in the work for the potential client.

A couple of weeks later, coincidentally on my five-year work anniversary, I asked if it was possible to include it on my expense report. Please note, I didn't put it on the report for reimbursement. Either way, I was ok. Instead of a simple "no" or a phone call, I was treated to a diatribe of text messages of how I didn't respect the company's money and was completely in the wrong. I quickly accepted the statement, but the abuse kept on coming my way, in the form of a 30-minute texting barrage. It was incredible that as the chief operating officer for a multi-million-dollar firm, I couldn't make a $150 decision. Even more surprising was I had been responsible for acquiring a large number of our revenue and delivering it profitably for years. It struck me that in my first job working for below minimum wage at a bike shop, I had been trusted with bigger decisions than $150, so I immediately decided to resign. A few months later, upon finding another role, it was my personal "iHop time" to move on to bigger things.

Saying Goodbye to Hollywood

As the song says, people will come in and out of your life, and this is certainly the case with situations and organizations. Here are some tips to help:

1. Hold onto your beliefs. Regardless of circumstances, if you don't know what these are, then take the time to write them down.
2. Realize regardless of your contributions, when it is time to move on, move on.

3. Always be networking! That doesn't mean you are actively looking for your next role, but these connections can be key to moving proactively or recovering quickly from an unanticipated job loss
4. Be prepared. Save for the possibility of being out of work
5. Compromise, as every job isn't the same. It is better to take new work than become a member of the long-term unemployed club. Once you start a new role, you have the opportunity to build skills and earn promotions.

In summary, maintain the awareness of whether it is iHop time or time to "Say Goodbye to Hollywood." The world holds countless opportunities, and it is perfectly fine to use your key to unlock yourself and move forward to the next adventure.

BEING "ALREADY GONE" AT WORK

The Eagles had the song "Already Gone" in which they sang about realizing they were free to leave a bad situation, and they were in control all along.[14]

The reality is in any organization, you need to keep a hint of attitude that you are "Already Gone." You maintain the choice of what is right for you in your life, and when the organization no longer wants you there, you need to be "Already Gone." You hold the key and don't need to be chained to others.

Stick to Your Word

I had joined a company as a vice president of finance for a region at the request of a new president of the region who wanted to shake things up. The last 18 months, I had been in a holding pattern at my last company in which I knew I was going to be laid off—along with 90%

of the staff—so I knew I was ready to do this. I joined the company and worked in Manhattan, which was exciting enough to make up for the long daily commute and long hours. The president and I began making changes, but about three months in, he decided he was getting too much resistance internally and resigned. This was a bad sign for me, but I was adaptable. I told myself it would all work out fine.

    The company appointed a third-generation employee as the new president, which wasn't a good sign for wanting change in the region. Meanwhile, I kept plugging ahead with changes in finance. A good example of the relatively minor change I made was in the efforts to collect money owed to us by customers. We had a massive amount of overdue money, so I hung up a dry-erase board with our collectors' names on it. I would have the collectors write the number of calls they had made at the end of each day. We set a target of 20 calls a day. Within a month, we had collected over 60% of the overdue money. This was millions of dollars in the bank with a minor change. The president called me into his office, and he told me he wanted to go back to the old way of collecting the money and disengage the extra efforts of the collectors. I swear I looked over my shoulder for a hidden camera thinking this had to be a practical joke he was pulling on me. Unfortunately, it was no joke. This pattern repeated itself for every change I made.

    Finally, after several months, I reached the point where it was clear it was time for me to move on, and I needed to be already gone. I approached him and simply said, "Look, it is clear you don't want a CFO or vice president of finance. You want an accounting manager. As I have zero desire to be an accounting manager, I think it is time we find a way to move on for our mutual benefit." He agreed, and we negotiated a relatively small exit package, as I had only worked there for less than nine months. Regardless, it was fair. The only other term of our verbal agreement was he would not disparage me to my employees or the larger team. I went to clean out my office, and we agreed the written agreement would be documented and signed in the next couple of days. I departed that afternoon and was ready to move on to looking for a new opportunity.

Later in the day, I got a call from one of my former employees. The president had immediately called a group staff meeting for my team, during which he brought up issues with me and implied I had been "let go for cause." Beyond the immediate feeling of being hurt by this, it dawned on me our agreement had not been signed yet. I called up the head of human resources and told her the agreement had already been broken, and therefore, I wanted double the exit package to sign. They really had no choice but to amend the agreement, and I moved on. This was all because the president could not keep his word until the agreement had been signed. Layoffs or leaving an employer are never easy, but why should you make them harder than they have to be? I was able to stay unemotional in this situation as I was already gone and had started exploring for my next opportunity.

The Semi-Annual Employee Purge

We had gotten to the point in which layoffs were so common that we (the survivors) had started calling them the "Semi-Annual Employee Purge." In fact, they became fairly commonplace, and we had gotten (somewhat) used to them. We all had to be ready and be already gone. However, this new layoff took on a whole different level of crazy!

It began on a quiet Thursday with an individual being called on the loudspeaker in the office to the HR VP's office. While they were in the office, the office manager scurried to the person's cubicle, emptied their belongings into a box, and greeted them when they returned. She immediately took their badge and escorted them out of the building. This went on person by person till about 5:00 p.m. at the end of a very long day. Some of us tried to hide in other places in the building and pretend our names weren't called. Those of us who were called were devastated. Those of us who weren't cut breathed momentary sighs of relief but then realized we could still be called. At the end of the day, most of us scurried out the door, simultaneously feeling survivor's guilt and happy to be leaving.

I stayed in the office a bit, quite frankly because I'd been so distracted by the trail of office supplies, tears, and gossip that I could not focus on my work. The VP of HR, who was a very experienced business executive and a solid citizen, walked with a stack of paperwork from his office, past my cubicle, and went into the CEO's office. He was only in there for about five minutes, and then he returned dejectedly to his office holding a single piece of paper. Was it a receipt for the signed paperwork? If not, then what was it? Was he dejected because he'd just laid off 40 people? That was understandable, but it seemed worse to me.

As the office was mainly empty, I stopped by to see him in his office. After some small talk, I asked him what had occurred. He said, "I went into the CEO's office and said, 'These are all the signed forms for the layoffs.' He looked at me and said, 'Not quite all' and pulled out my layoff notification for me to sign."

Yes, the CEO had made the VP of HR do the dirty work, then immediately afterward let him go.

Wow! Just, wow. Yes, he was let go, the exiting employees were treated disrespectfully, and the remaining staff was in a state of shock for weeks.

No Laissez-Faire with Layoffs

This, and many other events, have taught me there is a better way to handle employee layoffs. Among these are the following ideas:

1. Handle Exiting Employees Respectfully

    a. Go find them and bring them to your office for the conversation.
    b. Ask them if they have questions.
    c. Give them time to collect their things and say goodbye to their colleagues. They were trusted until the moment you notified them of their exit. Unless they have reacted in a violent fashion, there is no reason they can't have 15 minutes to clean out their desk themselves.
    d. Do not have someone else layoff the employee. It is your responsibility as the manager to do this and not delegate it to human resources. Human resources can attend the meeting but should not be having the primary discussion.

2. Treat the Survivors with Respect

    a. Hold a team meeting for the survivors to inform them of the reasons for the change and answer any questions. Do not hide in your office and leave the team wondering what will happen next.
    b. Give out new organization charts.

c. Reinforce an open-door policy for further questions.

Besides treating your employees more respectfully through layoffs, how do you treat yourself and be "already gone," as the song says? Here are some ideas:

- Be aware. Are leaders coming in and out of the organization like it has a revolving door?
- Think about the new leaders. Are they bringing good ideas, or are they taking the company backward? You are entitled to your opinion about the situation.
- Network. Keep in touch with others and be prepared to move on.
- Resume preparation is a good action. Update your resume annually. An even better step is to proactively update your resume in advance of the year's achievements. This helps you visualize the achievement and increases your chances to overachieve.

GO BE HAPPY SOMEWHERE ELSE

There was a song by Huey Lewis and the News called "Jacob's Ladder" in which they sing about getting stronger and better day after day.[15]

This is the attitude all employees should have, and sometimes getting better tomorrow means moving to be happy somewhere else. That's a natural aspect of life at work. Sometimes, the employee may need encouragement to leave. Regardless of the best efforts of recruiting a team and providing them training and feedback, sometimes the employee doesn't work out. It doesn't mean they are a bad person or worthless; it just means they aren't a good fit or used poor judgement. In those cases, I've found if the line is crossed, the employee is better off finding a role with another organization. They need to go be happy somewhere else—a place which is a better fit and a fresh start.

My Grandfather Is in the Hospital!

Jessica was a good employee I had recruited to do graphic design for the printshop I was managing. Beyond being good at her job—I knew this as I had filled in part-time for the role while it was vacant—she was always the first to volunteer to go make deliveries in our downtown area. Being chronically understaffed and without a delivery person, this was a great thing. Sometimes, it seemed as she was gone a bit long, but she still got her work done, and the rest of us didn't have to go make the deliveries.

One day, she got a telephone call, made a loud exclamation "My grandfather is in Central Hospital with a heart attack!" I told her to go, and we'd handle things in the store. The team briefly gathered around, and we couldn't do much, but we decided to send her grandfather some flowers. I ordered the flowers and set them up for delivery. An hour later, I got the call from the florist saying no such person was in the hospital. I confirmed his name and the hospital. However, the they still said the person wasn't there. Then, I called the other hospitals myself and got the same response from all of them. There was a mystery here, but I couldn't solve it alone.

When Jessica returned the next day, I brought her into my office and shut the door.

How is your grandfather doing?

He's recuperating, and it looks like he'll make a full recovery.

How was Central Hospital?

They really treated him right.

Good. Look, Jessica, we tried to send him flowers, and they said he wasn't in the hospital. In fact, he wasn't in any hospital in town.

Oh, they sent him home very quickly.

He had a heart attack, and within one hour of you getting the call, he was already sent home with no record of him?

Yes.

Jessica, why don't you tell me what was going on?

She still claimed she was telling the truth. I told her I knew she was lying, and this was the first strike and a verbal warning. If something like this happened again, I would write her up. Yet the mystery remained of what she was really doing. Was it a hot date? Did she just need a break in the middle of the day? It was really odd.

The mystery was solved the next week when she resigned and went to work for one of our customers. A different customer happened to let us know that while Jessica was out making deliveries, she was also hand-delivering copies of her resume to our customers. Her grandfather's heart attack was her excuse to leave to go on a job interview. Needless to say, I accepted her resignation and did not require her to serve out her two-week notice. She left that day. Perhaps my clear communication with her set the tone she needed to "go be happy somewhere else," and lying wouldn't be tolerated.

I Know How to Use a Gun!

Kelly was a new manager I had known for a few years. I was serving as an interim manager as her supervisor was out on maternity leave. She had an employee, Dor, who was basically ignoring her directions and any feedback she gave him. No matter how much coaching I gave her, she was getting absolutely nowhere with Dor. This was setting a bad example for rest of the close-knit team and also negatively affecting our ability to get our job done in a timely manner.

After several weeks, I decided to show Kelly how to hold these coaching sessions. We'd bring Dor into my office, and with Kelly in attendance, I would offer some coaching to him. Two birds with one stone. She'd see and hear firsthand how to provide the coaching from an experienced manager, and Dor would get the message. He would get back on track to being a productive employee. What could go wrong? By the way, don't ever ask that question!

Fast forward to the meeting, I began the coaching session. After offering Dor some initial feedback on areas for improvement, he responded with a tale of how he had served in the Israeli army and his proficiency with firearms! My initial, shocked reaction was to tell him I also knew how to use firearms. Please don't respond like that to an employee. My only excuse is I reacted in shock. Did he step back, apologize, and let the conversation get back on track? Absolutely not. He continued on the same track about his firearm expertise. At that point, I turned to Kelly, who had gone completely pale, and asked her to excuse Dor and me, but we had to go take the conversation elsewhere. I took Dor immediately upstairs to human resources, informed them he was essentially threatening us with guns in response to coaching, and he needed to be terminated. I made it clear Kelly was a witness to the event. Did he deny it? Not at all. End of story. They sat him down, terminated him, and escorted him quickly from the building. This was all because he couldn't accept relatively minor coaching on ways to improve. In that situation, he needed to go be happy somewhere else, and we needed to make sure our employees were safe.

Does He Know He's Been Fired?

Joe was a great new hire. He had passed the interview to be an acquisition assimilation manager with flying colors, and all of us were onboard with him joining the company. We were growing rapidly through acquisitions and needed help with someone to fly out on day one of the acquisition and help integrate the newly acquired firm into the parent company. He was knowledgeable and had zero trouble with lots of travel. After a couple of weeks of training, he took his first trip to Indianapolis. We were happy to have the help.

We got the phone call in the early afternoon of his first day on-site. It was the former owner of the business, and he was irate. He questioned what type of company we were if we would send someone like that to help them. We asked him to back up and tell us the whole story. There certainly was a lot to tell!

Joe had arrived onsite and immediately began hitting on the front desk receptionist. *Ok, that's not good, but we can manage the situation.* After several hours of meetings, during which he seemed distracted and would go off to talk to female employees while on breaks, they decided to take him for a tour of the Indianapolis Speedway. *Ok, we can deal with the distracted behavior. It will just take a quick conversation.* When they arrived at the Speedway, they went into the executive lounge, and there were beers available. Joe, to no surprise at this point, took two and drank them immediately. He then got two more as they proceeded to go see the track. Upon reaching the track, he was informed no alcohol was allowed, prompting him to chug back the two beers. They toured the track, and he got two more beers on the way back to the parking lot. Arriving at the former owner's new car, he was informed, "I don't let anyone eat or drink in my car." Any guesses on what happened next? Yes, he chugged both beers and threw the empty cups on the ground.

Well, it was clear that Joe, still very early in his probationary period, had three very large problems. One with treatment of fellow female employees, one with paying attention in meetings, and an apparent drinking problem. Bottom line was the controller, CFO, and I agreed he had to be terminated from his position before it got worse. Can you guess at this point it's going to get worse? Yup ... wait for it. He officially reported to the CFO, so he was tasked with terminating Joe. I called Joe and had him fly back to the home office. The next morning, he showed up, went into the CFO's office, was there about 15 minutes, and left the building. We checked in with the CFO, George, and he said everything went smoothly. Surprising, but the controller and I were happy it was over.

I was surprised when I got the call two weeks later from Joe informing me, he had had a very good, relaxing break and was ready to get back to work. Despite being incredibly confused, I told him I'd get some details and call him right back. Grabbing the controller, I went into George's office and asked, "What exactly did you tell Joe when you terminated him?"

George's response was "he needed some time off."

I asked, "Did you get his computer and badge?"

"No."

"Did you say, 'You're fired?'"

"No."

Ok, so now it was time to do two things. The controller practiced with George to say the words "you're fired," and I arranged for Joe to come into the office the next day and to bring his computer as we needed to do some software upgrades on it during his meeting. Joe arrived, and I greeted him, took his computer, and walked him to George's office. Five minutes later, Joe left without his badge or computer and was "really fired" this time.

Bend Over and Untie Your Boots

This one comes from my dad, the ever-practical Army physician's assistant. The Army scheduled sick call at the same time as physical training (PT) to not interfere with other duties of the soldiers and with the assumption that if they were sick, they should not be exercising anyway. The unforeseen consequence of this is sometimes soldiers would use sick call as a way to get out of doing PT. They'd go to sick call, get a prescription for something that would ideally stop PT for a week or so, and no one would be the wiser. That is except for a career Army PA who used to be a private in the Army.

 One day, a soldier came in complaining about an extremely sore back—So sore that he wasn't able to get any sleep and could barely move. He came walking in the exam room shuffling his feet slowing and holding his back. My dad showed complete empathy for the soldier's pain and promised to get to the bottom of it and get him feeling better. He could see the look of relief on the soldier's face. "Now, just untie your boots and get up on the table so we can get you better," my dad stated. The soldier bent over without hesitation, quickly untied his boots, and practically jumped onto the exam table. He didn't even see what was about to hit him. My dad calmly stated he was clearly faking his back injury, and he had the choice of immediately getting out of the office and back to PT, or he could perform the examination and then report him for lying to his superior officers. It would be the soldier's choice. According to my dad, the soldier couldn't have left the office any quicker if he'd been tied to a rocket. Hopefully, this allowed the soldier to see the error of his ways and not end up being dishonorably discharged from the Army.

Checking out of the Marriott

Although I did take the promotion to student manager at the Marriott in college to get out of the dish room, I also let the title go to my head a bit. Soon, I worked multiple shifts, late nights, and weekends—and even catered events at other schools. However, all of this work began to take its toll on my schoolwork, and my grades were dropping. My decision to have a conversation with my manager came after a really bad finals week in which I worked 55 hours filling in for absent managers who all had to focus on taking their own finals in five courses. I could barely see straight when the week ended, so I talked with Jerry and brought up my concerns. Naturally, he brought up my future career opportunities at the Marriott after graduation. However, I told him at this rate, I would be lucky to graduate. With a sigh of relief, we reached a compromise in which I would only work my scheduled shifts for the coming semester, and if they insisted on me working other shifts, I would quit on the spot.

After the winter break, students were back on campus, and we were starting to serve them food. I got a call on Sunday that another manager hadn't shown up, and they required me to come in immediately for the lunch service. I drove to the campus, turned in my name badge and food thermometer, and quit on the spot—exactly as we had agreed. They were stunned, but they were also in violation of our agreement. Quitting on the spot caused me some anxiety until I found another job, but it actually saved my college career, allowing me to graduate as scheduled.

No Help Needed

I had one of the rare occurrences of getting new, expanded responsibilities for a new team *and* getting time with their old manager, Mike, to transition the responsibilities. Mike and I met several times, and his responses and instructions were a bit vague. They were vague enough that I began to wonder how much Mike really knew about the work performed by these accountants. This was a bit disconcerting, but I kept working with him. We decided to divide up to work on some reports that were essential to the company in submitting official documents to the Securities and Exchange Commission. Billy, one of the employees, and I took on the U.S., which was 40% of the world. Mike and the rest of the team took on the rest of the countries.

Billy and I struggled with the report, and after two days, we were still off by $1 million. I asked Mike how they were doing, and he said they were done. He wanted our report, and "he would figure it out." Thankfully, in the spirit of training, I stayed with him to see how he solved the problem. He plugged the missing $1 million, hid it in the report, and sent it off to my boss. These are "go to jail" type of problems and not your local jail but Federal prison. I didn't pass out but went back to my office in private and called my boss. "I don't need Mike's help anymore during the transition."

"That's a surprise—why not?"

"Well, you got the report he just sent you? Open it up, please. See that place? He plugged it by a million dollars and you and I are going to be in a lot of trouble if we turn it in." Mike was immediately released from his duties, and we turned our attention to fixing the problem. Eventually, Mike left the organization entirely, and this was good for both the company and for Mike.

Help Guide Them to Their Happy

Underperforming employees happen. That's a guarantee. A sure sign of this is if they aren't "getting better than today," in the terms of the song. However, there are a few "best practices to help manage these situations:

1. Don't play ostrich! It is tempting to turn a blind eye to employee issues, but they rarely get better on their own. In fact, it's like the trash smelling bad, but rather than taking it out, you just ignore it. It doesn't smell better the next day. The problem won't solve itself.
2. Listen. Try asking questions and walking a mile in the shoes of the employee. This attempt may only last five minutes—but the reality is, the employee may have other issues going on outside of work and needs support.
3. Determine if more training and coaching will help the problem. Is there some knowledge the employee is lacking you can help with?
4. Try moving an employee to "cold storage". Sometimes, the employee isn't fitting in, and more training isn't a solution. However, you still have confidence they could be a good fit over time. In this case, you can solve it by moving them out of a customer-facing position and into "cold storage". Perhaps there is a special project, like conducting research or performing inventory, they could perform. I've had success with employees who have gone on to 20-year-plus careers with an organization once given some breathing room to get themselves on even footing.

5. Try the "you have two doors" strategy. In the event you know it isn't going to work (after steps 1–4, above), offer the employee two doors to choose from like in the old game shows. Set it up so they have the choice to make, and you are comfortable with whatever choice they make. Behind door one is their resignation, which can be dated to allow them the next six weeks of health benefits and a reference about duties performed in the job. Behind door two is the process of being written up three times and terminated on the third write-up. Write-up #1 will be given that day. Secondly, given their current performance history, the other two write-ups will occur by the end of the week. At that point, they will be terminated for cause. No severance, no extended benefits, and no neutral job reference. It is their choice. They can choose door one or door two. You are ok with either one but feel it would be best for all if they choose door one.

Not so top-secret information: They always choose door number one! They aren't bad people; they just aren't a good fit in the role or situation. People need the opportunity to "go be happy somewhere else." As the song says, "All I want from tomorrow, is to get it better than today," and we want that from employees—both those who stay and those who go.

THE FISH PRINCIPLE

Boston had the song "Rock and Roll Band," which included lyrics focused on having fun with their work.[16] We can't all be in a rock band, but just because you are at work doesn't mean you can't introduce fun into the environment for yourself, your colleagues, and employees.

What Water?

There's an old tale in which you ask a fish what it's like swimming in water. The fish replies "What water?" A fish doesn't think about the water they are swimming in. Rather, they are just doing their own thing in the way they know how. It is like that with us. Do we consciously think about walking around in all this air? What would our response be if asked about it? How does this apply to having fun in the workplace?

The reality is, we are all just swimming in the water we are in. We fall into patterns and approaches to problems and never think about the environment or if there is a different approach. We never ask, "What are we doing in this water?" or if we should even be in the water at all. Maybe we should be in the air or walking on land. You should consciously look at your work environment from this perspective. Are you doing things out of habit? Are there better ways to go about your work? Are there more ways to have fun in the workplace?

Tucson Toro's Spring Training

There is nothing better than minor league baseball with the exception of getting to see your favorite major league team, the Houston Astros, play their minor league affiliate, the Tucson Toros, as the culmination of spring training. In that case, you get a combination of the two!

My wife and I anxiously took our one-year-old son to the afternoon game, intending to watch our favorite players. After a few minutes, it was clear something was off. Jeff Bagwell didn't look like himself, despite wearing the jersey and crouching in his typical batting stance. Craig Biggio looked different too. He was much larger and broader in person than on TV. What was going on here?

It took another inning to realize what they had done. The Astros players had switched jerseys with each other and were impersonating the other players right down to the batting stances. No wonder Bagwell didn't look right. It was Biggio pretending to be Bagwell. Same thing with why Biggio looked broader. It was Bagwell pretending to be Biggio. My first reaction was to take offense. We had paid to see them play, and they were goofing around. But the second reaction was to see how much fun they were having as a team, with the Toros, and with the fans. They were having fun and blowing off steam in a game which truly had no long-term meaning. As a result, I've tried to keep the thought of finding a way to have fun at work even while working hard. People remember those times, and it helps you through the times when work can be painful.

The Financial Weather Report

Without a doubt, the most dreaded part of the annual company conference always occurred on day one during the opening remarks. After updates from the CEO and the discussions of marketing and sales came the financial update during which the information region by region for different financial results was presented, not discussed, to the audience. The only way it was survivable was if you handed out pillows for people to take naps! Believe me, this is coming from a finance guy's perspective. Painful doesn't do it justice. Being new to my role, I wondered how to make it better. I got with a friend in training, Steve, who was very creative with video presentations. We soon hit upon the idea of a "Financial Weather Report" we would pre-record and present at the conference. I would be the weatherman, and we would write a script that I would present in front of a green screen. We would add in weather maps of the country and world.

Soon, this evolved to the thought of having the *weather* change depending on the script. Yes, I was subjected to *raining* profits, *blowing* record sales, and a *chill* from the dropping profits in a region. We recorded it, and the presentation was a hit. The most boring, tortuous element of the presentation had the audience laughing and enjoying the themselves.

Sock-Em Boppers

Work is serious business and can get stressful. However, as a leader, it is important to find a way to burn off the stress and lighten the mood. I found our team in a stressful situation several years ago being overwhelmed with deadlines and layoffs. I decided to bring in "Sock-Em Boppers," which were essentially inflatable boxing gloves, and put them outside my office. People could put on one pair of gloves and hit a wall, or two people who were stressed out could each don a pair of gloves and fight it out to the laughter of both the crowd and each other. It was a cheap, easy way to have fun and burn off stress while under pressure.

Everyone, Please Celebrate Me!

This is an example of taking the idea of fun for your employees and making it all about you, the boss. To be clear, you should *avoid* this type of behavior. This is only fun for the leader.

    I was working for a large company that had just been acquired. The CEO from the acquiring company was coming to our office to walk around and introduce herself. That made a lot of good sense. However, it quickly took a turn down a bad path. The word got out that the CEO was touring the multi-building campus, and they had handed out clapping and cheering devices with the company's logo. Employees were expected to line the halls of the building to clap and cheer with the noisemakers when the CEO walked by. To me, this resulted in zero fun for the employees and turned the good idea of meeting the employees into an opportunity to feel celebrated by the employees. All the while, these same employees were unclear of what layoffs were going to occur in the future.

    Officially, I had to attend a conference call in my office and wasn't able to attend. I let the team know I would be otherwise occupied and wouldn't know if they attended.

It was up to their judgement on whether to attend the mini-parade through campus.

The FISH Principle[17]

There is an open-air fish market in Seattle that used to be a run-of-the-mill fish market. The new owner, however, had a habit of making it a fun place to work and inviting the customers to be part of the fun. Soon, the team made up chants and songs when interacting with customers. They even tossed fish over their customers heads to be packaged—all with smiles on their faces. What changed to make this fish market into a local tourist attraction? Did the fish suddenly stop smelling like fish? Were they no longer cold? Were the workdays shorter or new technology implemented? The answer to all of those questions is a resounding *no*. What changed was the *attitude*. They decided they would make it fun for themselves and their customers.

How can you make the fish model a reality during your day?

All jobs have stinky elements to them, yet if people working in a fish market can find a way to have fun and engage customers, you should look for a way to do the same.

Find a way to keep things light-hearted. Work through it. Calm down. Move on. Find your own way to enjoy what you are doing.

For example, I was working with a company that had a very disappointing year financially. Our monthly all-hands company meeting was coming up, and the CEO, CFO, and other senior executives wanted to skip the normal reporting of financial results because people might feel bad. My response, as the person responsible for the financial reporting, was people already knew the results were bad. People talked in the hallways, and there was no surprise about the issues we had faced all year long. We should speak to the results and then look forward to the new year and new results. Despite my attempts at persuasion, I went home the night before the meeting unsuccessful. I kept wondering if there was a different path. Was there a more fun way to acknowledge our issues and get over them? At home, I got out my guitar and quickly re-wrote part of the lyrics (in *italics*) to Jim Croce's "Working at the Car Wash Blues"[18] into something like this:

> Well, I had just got out of an *E.C. meeting, looking at the MRP*
> Tried to find some *more profits quickly*, but no matter how hard I *looked*
> They wouldn't listen to the fact that I was a genius
> The man says, "We got all that we can use"
> Now I got them steadily depressin', low down mind messin'
> *Underperforming blues*
> Well, I should be sittin' in an air-conditioned office in a swivel chair
> Talkin' *about how much money we're making*
> *Saying our stock will make us millionaires*
> Instead, I'm stuck here *cutting extra expenses*
> And *making cheaper travel plans*
> With them steadily depressin', low down mind messin' *underperforming blues*
> You know a place with our abilities, we should be smokin' on a big cigar
> But till *we* get *ourselves* straight, I guess *we'll all have*
> *To keep on driving our same old cars*
> Well, all I can do is shake my head

You might not believe that it's true
For workin' at *this NSC* is an undiscovered Howard Hughes
So baby, don't expect to see me with no *new Lamborghini*
Or new Italian suits
Cause I got them steadily depressin', low down mind messin'
Underperforming blues

I went in the next morning energized with a new plan. I quickly spoke to the CFO and explained my idea. This time, he agreed.

He opened the financial update portion of the meeting with "these financial results make me want to sing the blues. Does anyone else feel like singing the blues?"

I replied, "I do!" and went to get my guitar. We put the words on the screen, and I sang the song. I encouraged the team to sing along. By the end, we were all laughing and dealing with our results. The CFO stood back up, went through the results quickly, and focused us on our plan for the new year. We had faced our results but found a quick way to look forward to a new year.

Just like you can make yourself feel lousy, you can make yourself feel good and have fun at work

Making FISH Work for You!

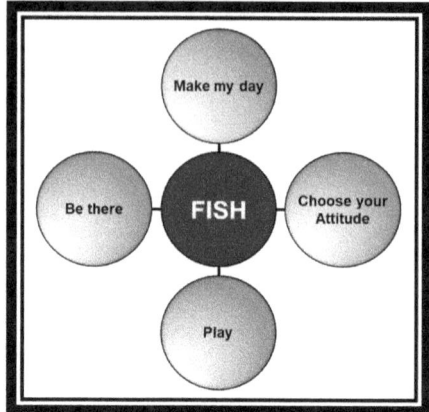

Think about these concepts in your office:

- What can you do to make your environment more fun?
- What can you do to make someone's day?
- What can you do to positively engage with your role and your customer?
- What can you do to *be there* at work and for your customer?

Develop a plan and introduce it to your team. Have fun in the workplace with your employees and customers.

IMPROVING THE WORK IN THE *WORK*PLACE

Working overnight and barely sleeping on the floor of your workplace is zero fun. I'll admit to veering toward overcompliance with rules when I was younger, but it came from wanting to accept the guidance of people who knew better. My company, which was very production-oriented, had a rule that said you needed to handle all of the work that came in during the same day. The concept was sound, as you would preserve production capacity for the next day if you produced every order you had received, regardless of the deadline. This worked really well because you did not know what new orders would come in the next day, and if you had work queued up in production, you might have to say no to new, emergency work. This would decrease your sales.

Taking this very literally rather than conceptually, the next thing I knew, I was understaffed and working overnight in downtown Austin while sleeping for an hour or two on the grey carpet in the back room. It took me some time to find flexibility in the rules and realize a hiring freeze that kept us at a 50% staffing level wasn't consistent with wiping the slate clean. During this very long six-week period, I realized this and kept interviewing for new staff, regardless of the hiring freeze. Finally, although the freeze wasn't lifted, headquarters announced we could fill out forms to request exceptions to the freeze. Broken from overcompliance with the rules, I filled out the forms for three exceptions and faxed them to headquarters. I waited five minutes and then faxed in three sets of new hire paperwork for my new team members. Legally, headquarters couldn't un-hire people from 1,000 miles away. I technically followed procedures but in a way that would empower my team to achieve the results in a more efficient and effective way. The concept is good to preserve capacity but not in an ineffective manner.

YOU'LL END UP JUST LIKE RICKY THE GOAT!

Dire Straits performed a song called "Money for Nothing," which included the lyrics about how easy it appeared to be a rock star rather than working daily jobs.[19]

The band contrasted the life of everyday people from rock stars offering how much easier the lives of rock stars were. In this chapter, we'll talk about the benefits of double-checking your work, working more efficiently, and becoming more of a rock star.

My First Real Job!

"I can hire you but only for $2 an hour cash—if you start right now!" Sal said to me. I was 16 years old and desperate for a job in a small town overrun with teenagers looking for jobs. So, I started right there at the bike shop in downtown Ozark, Alabama, working for an ex-Navy guy named Sal who had a very colorful vocabulary. I destroyed my white shirt on the first day as I climbed in the loft to haul out old bicycles covered with grease and dust. But at the end of each two-and-a-half-hour shift, he would pull out a $5 bill and give it to me. It was a start, and I was no longer mowing yards outside in the Alabama heat!

The biggest thing Sal taught me was how to work efficiently. He had zero tolerance for inefficient work. For example, if I picked up a box to move to a new location, I'd have to set it down to clear a place for it. "Why did you do that?" he would shout from across the store. "Now, you are picking up the box twice! Always clear a space first, then only pick up the box once!" Over and over through the year I worked there, he reinforced the same message to work more efficiently without making messes for myself or others. To this day, I think about how to move something more efficiently and "not pick up the box twice." This applies to whether it is physical labor or the work required to do research or write reports. There is a sequence that makes the most sense, and I try to use that most of the time.

Zero-Basing

One way of working more efficiently is to get rid of the accumulation of gunk that builds up in a business over time. This can be old policies and practices that are no longer necessary. An example I heard of recently is an old law in South Carolina that prohibits having horses in bathtubs.[20] I don't even want to know where it came from; however, it makes you wonder what equivalents you may have in your organization.

Zero-basing is basically just starting with a blank piece of paper or blank white board and drawing out the way you would do it today without the legacy of the past.

Oftentimes with clients, I discover the current practices are such a mess that it is a waste of time to document them and then find ways to improve. We are better off just gathering a group of people and starting from zero. Think about this when trying to improve your organization: you can improve efficiency quickly by starting over.

Leaning toward Sawyer's

Language is an odd thing, particularly when you move around a lot with your family and have your own use of language no one else on the planet uses. It felt even worse because I didn't realize it was my own language until after I became an adult. Using your own language others don't understand can definitely lead to inefficiency in the workplace. Let's lay out just a few of these:

Phrase	Meaning	Origin
Dark over Willy's mother's house	A Bad Storm is coming	Grandfather in Montana where the storms always came in from one direction—from his friend Willy's house
Bat out of Bennet	Driving really fast	A Southern Baptist clean-up of dirty language ... after all, you couldn't say "Bat out of Hell"
Snuck up on my blind side while I was shucking these peas	Expressing surprise	Small town Alabama from a local who we surprised outside a gas station

It's time for Gwilly	Time to go to bed	Welsh ancestor's phrasing
That's why I voted for you, Stanley	I agree with you	From "Seems Like Old Times"
Let Polly do the printing	Let someone else better suited do the work	From "Jaws"
42	Answer for almost any question	From *The Hitchhiker's Guide to the Galaxy* as the answer to the question of Life, the Universe, and everything
Gobsmacked	Shocked or surprised	English phrase
You might want to let that breathe awhile …	Pause for a few minutes	From Jaws when they open a bottle of wine and immediately start drinking it
Buggeration	What in the world!	English phrase
Gruntled	Satisfied	A real English word that has fallen out of favor; the opposite of disgruntled
Grins and giggles	Happy times or "just because"	A cleaned up Southern Baptist version of "Shits and giggles"

Leaning toward Sawyer's	Something is crooked or leaning sideways	A barn in the dairy in Maine leaned to one side—toward the Sawyer farm
Might as well, we can't dance!	Let's do it, there's nothing else to do!	The conservative, southern college my parents went to did not allow dancing. Shorthand when someone wanted to do something was "Might as well, we can't dance!"

Even "It's iHop Time" and "Go Be Happy Somewhere Else" used in this book exemplify the point. Can you imagine me speaking to other humans and using these phrases? There's only a couple that might be understandable, and then people would just think I'm a moron who doesn't know the right phrase.

Do you find yourself using your own vernacular with your employees or clients? Sometimes, this can be throughout an organization, company, or department but leads to confusion when talking with the outside world. Work to be more aware of your own language and adapt to talking in a way understandable to more people or be aware enough to explain your phrasing. This extra work will make you more efficient in the workplace.

Don't Be Like Ricky!

"Did I ever tell you about my goat, Ricky?" The question took me completely by surprise as the CFO and I were reviewing a spreadsheet I had prepared. "No" was my simple response, but inside, I was wondering where this was going.

I was a (mostly) self-taught finance guy working for a division of a major, publicly traded company. My boss, Larry, was not a native Texan, but he got there as soon as he could. I was still not 30, while he was nearing 50 with lots of experience. Though I was learning quickly, I had some bad habits, one of which was hard-coding numbers where formulas should be making the spreadsheet have errors if something changed. This is a big problem when people are counting on accuracy, so building inefficiency and mistakes is a bad approach.

Larry proceeded to tell me about how, as a child, he had a goat named Ricky who would constantly get loose, jump the fence, and begin having intercourse with the female goats. They tried a taller fence, but it did not work. They added barbed wire at the top, and it didn't work. Finally, they tied Ricky with a rope far too short to jump over the fence. That would surely work.

Mid-story, I am listening but lost. Where could this possibly be going?

So, one day, Larry came home and found out that Ricky had stretched the rope enough to leap over the barbed-wire fence but not enough to clear it. Instead, he had caught his testicles on the fence and was stuck at the top. Larry quickly turned to me and said, "And if you hard-code anything in a spreadsheet again, you'll find yourself just like Ricky!"

Yes, the CFO had just found a very creative way of breaking a bad habit. Yes, I think he threatened me with castration, but the lesson was learned, and it broke my inefficient, error-prone bad habit. Permanently.

Warning: Don't Do It!

I was with the client we had been working with for almost six months, and we had created a very good business case for a transformation project for the finance department for the company. There had been some internal resistance, but at the end, we had a conservative, achievable business case. Our original numbers were almost unbelievable, showing almost $80 million in annual savings, so we had made the numbers increasingly more conservative, ending with a $24 million savings number and a reasonable payback period and return on investment.

This client was privately owned by the founder of the organization, so we knew every dollar we asked them to invest was like asking the founder to take money out of his wallet. Therefore, we took the $4 million investment number very seriously. However, I could sense the reticence of the company's project manager as we were finishing this phase (and hoping to win more work). I instinctively knew what he was thinking. Turning to him, I said, "Don't do it!"

He said, "Don't do what?"

"Don't make the business case more conservative. We've already done that," then I walked him through the steps. He was still reluctant to commit to the large $24 million savings number. To which I said, "If you don't get these costs under control, when the owner dies, the company will be sold to the highest bidder—and there will be blood in the streets from the number of people they cut." I was advocating that by taking the actions proactively, they could remain in control.

Fast forward two months, and I received a phone call. "Can we talk for a bit?" Sure enough, they had presented a business case That offered zero—yes, *zero*—cost savings for a $4 million investment and were stunned it was turned down. They asked us to help fix the situation, and it was basically unfixable. It would be one thing to make a number more conservative, but by taking the number down to zero, they were backed into a corner. Any savings numbers greater than zero now looked like they were invented to get the owner's approval rather than being generated through a thoughtful process. Our whole process had been made completely inefficient and wasteful by not avoiding the situation.

Avoiding Barbwire Fences

Speed is good, but moving too quickly can lead to trouble, and you don't want to get a lecture like I got from Larry! You won't feel like you are getting your "Money for Nothing!" Here are some steps to make sure you manage your speed:

1. Breathe! Slow down and understand the objective.
2. Ask yourself (or someone else) questions, such as "will the work need to be modified or used again?"
3. Double-check your work. If I had tested the spreadsheet Larry convinced me not to hard-code, I would have found my error. It would have only taken five minutes longer to test and fix the problem.

Conservativism, in my last example is also good—but it can cost you time and money. Here are some steps to manage conservatism:

1. Be transparent in your thinking. We probably should have disclosed the original business case and walked them through the step-by-step process of

making it more conservative. In that way, it would have been more believable. Perhaps they would have avoided the temptation of making it more conservative.

2. Tell the client or your boss, as the case may be, what they *need* to hear, not what they *want* to hear. In this case, I handled it correctly by making the horrifying statement that there would be "blood in the streets." They didn't want to hear it, but they needed to hear it. When I last spoke to them, years later, they still had not achieved the changes they desired, all while spending the worldwide budget for a technology solution that would only work in the U.S.

3. Try to fix it. If you have been too conservative, make the attempt to fix it.

WORK UNTIL YOUR WORK REACHES ITS LOGICAL CONCLUSION

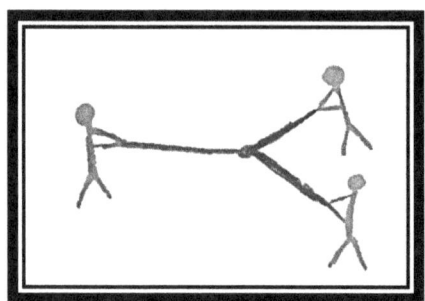

The Billy Joel song "Pressure" has lyrics that speak to not understanding pressure until you are truly in difficult situations.[21]

How does this relate to leadership and the workplace? We all have time pressures and work production pressures with deadlines, bosses, and objectives. How do you manage the workload, and how can you handle the pressure?

The Logical Conclusion of Your Work

At one time, after a number of company restructurings and layoffs, I ended up having three direct supervisors in three different departments. No, two of them were not dotted-line managers. All three were vice presidents, and I had a solid line reporting relationship to each of them—one in finance, one in operations, and one in special projects. Even I could see what was going to happen, but apparently, they did not see it coming. Each, without coordinating with the other, would come to me for work with individual deadlines and priorities. Naturally, these individual workloads and deadlines would overlap each other and cause pressure. Over several weeks, night after night, I would go home having missed deadlines and caused disappointment for one or more of my supervisors. I eventually asked the VP of special projects how to handle the situation. His answer: "Work until your work reaches its logical conclusion." I stood there in the office, dazed and confused. To use the British term, I was gobsmacked. What was that supposed to mean? How was I to use that to improve my productivity? To be honest, his advice, at the time, really did not help me at all to relieve the pressure I felt. I simply held on and worked more hours to get the work done.

Several years later, I was working on my MBA while working a full-time job. Both work and schoolwork felt overwhelming. Handling two to three classes and having a full-time management role felt worse than the three supervisors. It was then I finally discovered what my supervisor in Tucson was trying to tell me to better manage pressure. There are only so many hours in the day to get work done. You need to realize that not all of your work can be A+ work, and some just has to reach its logical conclusion so you can move on to other work. I began the practice of setting endpoints for work and then spending 30–45 minutes polishing the work product. Once polished, I would send it on, either to professors or to my supervisor at work, and then get some sleep. I learned an A was still an A, and it was ok if it was not an A+. The objective was to get the work done and move forward. It was not to create perfection in all things. Once I learned to deal with the pressure, my grades and work performance actually improved dramatically from those in the past.

How Many Name Changes Are Enough?

One branch of my family had a particular way of saying exactly what they thought to whoever was around. It didn't matter if they were talking with royalty or country officials. They did not handle pressure with a lot of tact. This branch goes back quite a way, with some of the relatives serving in official roles during the time of Joan of Arc. The family was well-established with the name DuGuesclin and even had a family crest. However, they ran into trouble in France and left. Trouble in England followed, and the family finally ended up with the Dutch. They basically left each country on the run from officials. They eventually settled on the name Goslin when they came to live in the New York area when it was New Amsterdam and owned by the Dutch. This worked pretty well for a generation, but then the Dutch sold the land to the English. One older ancestor *had* to leave due to his conflict with the English and ended up living out his life in St. Croix. The rest of the family stayed and went about their business, having apparently learned their lesson about getting in trouble with the authorities and managing high-stress situations.

Many years later, the American Revolution broke out, and they were encouraged to join the troops under General George Washington. They basically told the folks to do what they wanted to do, but they weren't going to get involved in the fight. Their approach had morphed into avoiding conflict to manage pressure. Ironically enough, having learned their lesson in some ways, they were branded as Tories, or English Loyalists, and kicked out of the newly formed United States of America and had to flee to Canada. Only at the beginning of the 20th century did the family re-immigrate to the US and with one more name change to Gosline, just to be safe.

I Don't Know Their Name!

We had a major client we worked with for about a year and half, and it worked well. We were brought in by the CFO to evaluate how the team was functioning, and the work was very interesting. The only significant challenge was the organization's CEO couldn't decide if he agreed with the organization structure. Literally, in the course of a ten-story elevator ride, my team felt the pressure and confusion build up as he would shift from agreeing to the structure to wanting to blow it up by shifting all the work back to their businesses from the CFO and headquarters. The same thing repeated itself numerous times with no real resolution.

After we ended our phase of work, I lost touch with the CFO—due mostly to my surgery—and I only recently got back in touch with him. I discovered the old CEO had departed, and a new one joined the company. This new CEO didn't know the name of our firm, so he didn't trust our work. Instead, he dictated to the CFO to bring in one of the big four consulting firms. Not only did they validate that our work formed a very good foundation for the organization, but the new CEO quickly departed the organization completely. The CFO is still there, and we are discussing possibilities of working together again. I learned two things. One, we had managed the confusing, stressful situation well and performed high-quality work, and two, we couldn't control the opinions of other people.

Two Men out and Three on Base

As the song states, sometimes the "Pressure" is immense. It falls on your shoulders like it up to you to win a baseball game. Here are some steps you can take to manage being jammed with pressure-filled deadlines and competing priorities:

1. List out the tasks and deadlines.
2. Determine the priorities and decide whether you can meet the deadlines.
3. Ask for clarification. Many times, I've made assumptions while working independently and trying to guess what was wanted and when. Don't repeat this mistake.
4. Ask for help. Don't complain about the work, but if you have determined the deadlines and priorities and still can't produce the work, then don't be afraid to ask for assistance and support (or reprioritization).

The key is not perfection. The key is not making the pressure go away. The key is finding your own way to deal with the pressure and achieve success (and still get some sleep)! Once you find this key, I wouldn't be surprised if your outputs and results actually improve dramatically.

MISTAKE-PROOFING

"Landslide" became a huge hit for Fleetwood Mac, and it was written by Stevie Nicks. The lyrics speak of being afraid of change in difficult circumstances.[22]

In this case, we want to manage unplanned changes and get bolder by mistake-proofing our work to make the basic elements better all of the time.

Stuck at an Airport

I was exhausted from nearly a month of travel and found myself stuck with a delayed flight on the other side of the country from home. On a positive note, however, it looked like the flight would be nearly empty. Only one older man and I sat waiting for the flight. I had reached the point after six months of near-constant travel to just sit and wait. However, the gentleman got up and went to the desk to ask about the flight status. "We will know more in about 30 minutes, Mr. Deming," the attendant responded. Deming? Is that why his face looked familiar? I looked at him more closely as he came back to his seat. Older, yes, but familiar. He was *the* Deming of the "Total Quality Management" movement. He was the man brought to Japan by General MacArthur, the man with the reputation of rebuilding the Japanese manufacturing environment after World War II.[23] Yet here he was, stuck in the airport, the same as I.

I couldn't resist introducing myself, and we began to have a conversation. None of the big stuff about his past was discussed. I felt like he probably got more questions in this vein than he wished for on a daily basis. The topic was more about how he wanted to finish his trip and get home to D.C. However, I couldn't resist asking him about the irony of being stuck in an airport due to a quality issue with an airplane. His response struck a chord with me. "You have to embrace quality and make it part of your day-to-day operations. It isn't something you do once, and it works. This airline talks about quality—but doesn't live quality. That is the issue."

Does your company *talk* rather than *do* quality? Are its actions integral with its words?

Sandwich Shop, Baskets, and Trash Cans

Several years ago, a sandwich shop faced a problem costing them employee time and money. They served their sandwiches in plastic, reusable baskets. The company had to make constant changes to avoid losing the baskets. They asked their customers to make sure to *not* throw away the baskets but place them next to the trash cans. That didn't work. They put signs up to remind the customers ... and again, this didn't work. Trash cans were filled with the baskets, and the company kept spending more money buying replacement baskets.

The company's next solution was to have their employees spend time digging through the trash bags to retrieve the lost baskets. It was not a safe or fun task for their employees.

The solution eventually came through changing the trash cans. By changing the opening to be smaller than the basket, it was *impossible* for customers to throw away the reusable baskets. There was no choice but to set the basket aside. This immediately took the compliance rate to 100%, eliminating lost baskets and employee time spent digging through the trash. Plus, no more changes were required.

This is a very simple form of mistake-proofing. By making it impossible for a mistake to occur (in this case, throwing away the basket), you eliminate mistakes and all of the consequences of those mistakes.

How to Mistake-Proof

Think about what areas you can avoid constant change in by mistake-proofing your business:

1. Brainstorm the areas that cost you the most time or have the lowest quality (or the most rework) in your business.
2. Ask your employees about their jobs and the mistakes they make on a daily basis.
3. Reward your employees for bringing up mistake-proofing possibilities and implementing them in the workplace.
4. Hold mini-workshops over lunch or have an early breakfast to develop ways to mistake-proof areas of your business.

DON'T BE DUMB

Led Zeppelin had a hit with the song "Fool in the Rain," which when summed up, has the main character waiting for a date in the rain and getting stood up.[24] At the end of the song, we learn he is on the wrong block. Often, businesspeople behave the same way, sitting around and complaining about things that are not making sense while making a fool of themselves for not solving their problems ... or eliminating dumb activities.

Eliminate S.T.U.P.I.D.

A colleague and I developed a program with minor success called "Eliminate S.T.U.P.I.D." in which the letters stood for:

    S—Slow
    T—Tedious
    U—Un

P—Productive (as in "Unproductive")
I—Inefficient
D—Duplicative

The program was designed to get the team to find work processes that did not make sense nor did it make it better. However, aside from a few responses, it was met with limited positive results. Of course, this is the same colleague who when he saw the phrase "faster, faster till the thrill of speed overcomes the fear of death" loved it. We loved it so much we had it printed on polo shirts for the whole team. Though, we didn't anticipate employees would interpret them to mean we wanted to work themselves to death. When they became nicknamed "the death shirts," we knew we had taken a wrong turn.

At my next company, I decided to try again but with a better developed program. This time, I did the following:

- Developed a sign for the hallways and cubicles that looked like the following:

- Developed a S.T.U.P.I.D. Sighting Report, including a one- to two-sentence summary of the issue, a one paragraph description of the problem, and a one-paragraph idea for how to "Eliminate S.T.U.P.I.D."
- Built an incentive program with a $5 Starbucks gift card for every idea received.

- Held a team kick-off meeting and required each individual to submit two S.T.U.P.I.D. sightings.

What were the results?

- Received nearly 100 sightings in one week
- Hung them on the wall
- Attacked the areas with strong opportunity—marked out with a red sign when eliminated and gave the individual another reward and recognition in the monthly group meeting

How did the results change?

We found overwhelming success in S.T.U.P.I.D. sightings with a wide range of areas to pursue. The first issue we attacked was one in which our company was writing checks to ourselves. I realize this sounds unbelievable, but this is exactly what made it S.T.U.P.I.D. Here is a summary of the issue:

- They had acquired another company a couple of years before, but the acquiring company was still writing checks to the acquired company with a number of offices in the northeast U.S.
- These offices would then receive the checks by mail.
- No longer having bank accounts, they would express mail the checks to the regional office outside of Boston.
- Once per month, the Boston office would express mail the checks to Houston (at an office one-quarter of a mile from the department who had originally mailed the checks).

- My employee would open the envelopes, code the amounts, and drive to the local bank to manually deposit these checks.
- Given the multiple express mailing charges, time, and mailing of the original checks, time in coding and depositing the checks and the fact that the accounting was wrong for a publicly held company, there was quite a lot of S.T.U.P.I.D. in this item.

What were the results?

Eliminating writing checks to ourselves was the first task out of the 100 items we attacked as a management team to save time and money for the company. Additionally, we recognized the employees who identified items we resolved and freed capacity for the team to do work with more meaning. We enjoyed another additional benefit: when the organization went through layoffs, our team was absorbed the work from other departments without needing addition team members or overworking our team.

The human resources department was a bit horrified when they heard the name and wanted to rename it "Get SMART." In fact, another team tried the same program with the new name and failed miserably. I think the politically incorrect name caused it to get attention and focus breaking through the noise of the daily work environment.

How to Eliminate S.T.U.P.I.D.:

Decide you aren't going to be dumb—or act like the "Fool in the Rain." Instead, follow the recipe for what worked for the second time I implemented the idea:

- Develop a S.T.U.P.I.D Kit.

- o   Sign for the hallways and cubicles
- o   S.T.U.P.I.D. Sighting Report *(See appendix for a sample)*

- Build an incentive program, something of nominal value to recognize your employees.
- Hold a team kick-off meeting and require each individual to submit two S.T.U.P.I.D. sightings.
- Post all the ideas to the wall ideally where the whole team can see them.
- Review the ideas and prioritize ones that give you quick wins.
- Implement a few quick wins.
- Mark them off on the wall.
- Recognize the individuals in your next group meetings.
- Repeat as necessary to make your organization more effective and efficient.

BRING ON THE DYNAMITE! — REMOVING OBSTACLES AT WORK

Operations manuals became second nature to me after a couple of years. There was one way to do things, and it was all documented for anyone to look up. It didn't matter if you were in East Brunswick, New Jersey, or opening a new location in Moscow. You followed the manual. You would think this would shut down innovation and new thinking. After all, it sounds like working on an assembly line in which thinking isn't allowed. However, by removing the need for you to think about every activity, you actually free up time for new solutions to new problems. An example of this was a store I worked with in Denver.

They followed our program and procedures exactly as recommended for operations, finance, and sales. As a result, they broke sales and productions records by three months after opening their location. The program was working on a day-to-day basis. However, their rapid growth did uncover a weakness we had never seen. They were running out of cash because their sales were so high. Vendors and employees had to be paid, but they had not collected their cash from the large sales. We found a solution by focusing more efforts on collecting from customers. The other processes were essentially on autopilot, which freed capacity for developing a new solution to a new problem. Which of your processes can you put on autopilot and do the same way every time? This makes it easier to delegate work and train your team. It also will, paradoxically, lead to more time for creative solutions.

MAINTAIN THE BUNGEE-CORD APPROACH

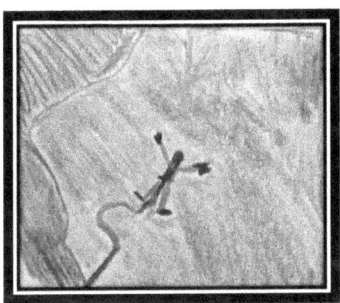

Todd Snider recorded a song called "Statistician's Blues," which, after going into details about statistics in excruciating detail, goes on to say there is too much to think about and feeling stuck between hope and doubt.[25]

You can get stuck in the details so much that it makes you want to have a drink and gives you too much to think about. How do you deal with this situation?

It's Bus Time

Recently, my team and I were working on a project with a state bus service and tasked with understanding what was happening in their money rooms (where they counted the money from the buses) and make it a better situation for all. We immediately saw that the best plan was to go beyond talking to only one or two of the money rooms; we also needed to go across the state to talk to all the personnel. Rather than stay in a conference room and talk to the managers, we were diving in the detail by talking to the entire team. How did we maintain our objectivity and not drown in the detail? We created a standardized checklist to follow in our conversations with the team.

By the morning of day one, we also realized we needed to understand where the money was collected, and we needed to go on the buses. The staff was shocked when we asked to see this. We soon understood why. None of them had ever physically been on one of the buses. Did we spend a lot of time on the buses? Not at all. We didn't lose ourselves in evaluating the buses or give ourselves too much to think about. Instead, we stayed focused and pulled ourselves back out of the detail after a few minutes. However, focus on details gave us a lot of insight into issues occurring in the money rooms, and we were able to share that information with the staff.

New Computers via the Rental Car Express

Isn't it odd for a computer company to find their staff with old, inadequate computers? And even more odd, I've seen computer and technology companies without the ability to order new computers.

I found myself with a new team of employees after a merger that included teams on both sides of San Francisco Bay. I'd been trying for a couple of months to get the team on the west side of the bay better computers but to no avail. I went out to visit and confirmed face to face they needed new computers during my visit.

The next day, I drove the rental car to the team on the east side of the bay. Beyond introducing myself and learning more about their responsibilities, I discovered they had a room full of old computers that had been replaced. I realized something even more surprising:

these old computers were several years newer than the ancient machines the west bay team was using. I dove into the details and decided to load the computers into my rental car, filling up the trunk, backseat, and passenger seat. Then, I drove them back across the bay. What did I accomplish other than breaking the official rules on computer procurement? We freed up space in the storage room at the east bay location, and I demonstrated to my team that leadership was interested in solving their problems and dealing with consequences later. I made sure I was the only one to load and unload the computers. This gave each team deniability to the event. This also gave me and my team one less thing to think about daily.

Rebuilding the Cubicles

After going through several rounds of what we called the semi-annual employee purge, more conventionally known as layoffs or right-sizing, the company headquarters was a mass of empty cubicles where my former co-workers had sat. About half of the workforce was gone, and no one had made any effort to relocate the remaining employees into one area or to dismantle the empty workspaces. Let's face it—it is never easy to come to work when you are missing the people you used to work with. It is even worse when you arrive at work each day and see their empty workspaces as you walk to your cubicle.

After several weeks of this, I took a look at the cubicles and realized they were easily reconfigured using an axle wrench. A plan was formed! The following weekend, I came into the office and reconfigured several cubicles, essentially giving the remaining employees more space while eliminating the empty cubicles. I went home quickly, as I couldn't fix it all or remain stuck in the details of something that wasn't my responsibility.

On Monday morning, everyone arrived and, rather than asking questions, just assumed the company had reconfigured the cubicles. Although I could see the look of confusion on the office manager's face, I was determined not to say anything unless asked. The team was happier and more satisfied, and you could feel an increase in the energy of the office.

I'll See You in the Office Tomorrow

"What do you mean you'll see us in the office in New Delhi tomorrow? You aren't scheduled to be here for another three months." Yes, I surprised the team in India, and I had just booked a flight from New Jersey to fly there overnight. They didn't realize I had a ten-year business visa to India and always had a suitcase in the trunk of my car. I had just spent the last week being told "yes" to changes that needed to be made, but I was seeing no action or results. When I worked with folks at great distances, they felt they could manage me and my expectations. However, a deadline was coming up, and I wasn't promoted to this role to maintain the status quo. I was hired to make things better. It was time to dive in the details.

After a long flight to India, I was greeted by a nervous team. However, by getting in a conference room face-to-face, we not only solved the problems and improved things, but I also sent them the message that I was willing to fly around the world at the drop of a hat if necessary. This helped us drive things forward and make great improvements in the next several months, and that hard work allowed us to sell off the operation to a third party at a profit.

Zero to Worry about in Payroll

Well, that was certainly good news to hear, I thought to myself. I was asked to take a role for a person who had joined five months prior and seemed to be running out of the building very rapidly. Never a good sign. However, with operations in a lot of areas, it was good to hear payroll was functioning well. They had just implemented the function and hired a new staff five months prior, so it was a surprising bit of good news.

However, having been well aware of the nuclear disarmament talks in the 1980s where the phrase "trust but verify" was used to mean we should trust others to disarm but then inspect the missile silos to make sure they were really empty, I didn't want to assume all was well.

I went to meet the five-person payroll team and introduce myself. After a round of introductions, I asked one simple question, "Can I see your manual check log?" You see, if things were running smoothly, there would be little activity needed in writing manual checks to fix mistakes. I took a quick look and noticed something was awry. They had written over 1,500 manual checks in five months equating to more than one manual check for every U.S. employee in the company. Quickly validating I was reading the numbers correctly, I asked, "Why are you writing these manual checks?" The reply was stunning. "Our previous manager told us to do whatever human resources wants done ... so that's what we've been doing." A-ha! There was the reason for why there was no need to worry about payroll. Any mistakes made by human resources (like approving timecards or adding new employees) were being covered up when HR asked for a manual check to fix the mistake. No employee complaints led to zero issues for HR.

Resolving this situation happened in two steps. First, I went to the head of human resources and informed her we were no longer writing manual checks *without* having the requestor talk to me first. She accepted this, as I was still willing to write the checks. Second, I took each and every phone call over the next month, listening and asking detailed questions. This was quite an investment in time for an area that had "zero issues." I approved each check so as to not penalize the employee for HR not doing their job correctly, but the HR representatives no longer wanted to talk with me. Therefore, they started doing their job correctly. After a month, our manual checks dropped to three for the month down from an average of 300 per month, and I moved back out of the details having improved the lives of the payroll department and eliminating unnecessary work and cost.

The Last-Minute Sri Lankan Tourist

I realized at the end of a huge project moving work to a third-party in Sri Lanka that there was no way to dive in the details and validate the work would be performed correctly. The outsourcer was new to the work, and this client was their first in the non-governmental organization (NGO) world, and they promised everything would be fine. However, the previous transitions had not gone smoothly, and there was a lot of noise that said things weren't happening correctly with the other regions. In fact, that was why my external team had been called in to help with the transition of the final and largest region.

This required me to go to Sri Lanka in the final two weeks of the project with zero planning to make the trip. This isn't usually a big deal for a quick trip from the U.S. However, when I looked up the business visa requirements, they required several forms and several weeks of processing time. There wasn't an expediting service. It just took more time than I had available. However, by looking at the details on their website, I did find a tourist could travel to Sri Lanka and just apply as they entered the country for a tourist visa. It was really the only option I could find.

I went to the airport in my shorts and Hawaiian shirt, doing my best impression of an American tourist. My suitcase was mostly loaded with casual clothes. Yes, I took my laptop, but this was a requirement if I was called for any projects while out of the country. I half-expected to get to the front of the customs line and get turned back. However, I passed into the country and got to spend a week working in the office making sure all of the details were put in place. I also saw some interesting tourist sites like the beach in Colombo during my trip. I still need to go back to see the elephants, though!

Avoiding Quicksand

How do you dive in the details but avoid the issues of having too much to think about? There are a number of ways to handle these situations. These include

1. Realize a task can't be delegated and why. This avoids the temptation to always be in the detail and not properly delegate to your team.
2. Create a mental image to avoid getting stuck in the detail. I imagine myself tied to a bungee cord. I'll drop into the detail but be pulled up quickly.
3. Teach your team the same approach.

BRING ME A CALCULATOR!

Bob Seger had the song "Old Time Rock and Roll" in which he reminisced about the past and talked about appearing old-fashioned.[26]

Sometimes, as in the examples below, being a relic or old-fashioned is the quickest way to solve the problems at hand.

Rockingham as a Secret Code

My grandfather ran his shoe store with almost no technology. This shouldn't be too surprising as he got his start in business after leaving high school early to earn money during the Great Depression. After a successful career with Belk's, a regional department store, he didn't want to move his family again, so decided to strike out on his own.

I was always surprised when he would either mark down types of shoes for sales or negotiate on the fly with customers buying shoes for the whole family to reduce the price. How did he know he was making money and not selling at a loss? Did he somehow have the prices of hundreds of pairs of shoes memorized? He had no computer, just a simple cash register. He would *never* go back to a report or invoices before reducing the prices, and he always made money. It was quite a mystery.

Robert's grandparents in front of their shoe store

One vacation when I was working a part-time job and helping with the store when I visited him, I had gained enough business knowledge to ask him to explain what he was doing and what his secret was to the price reductions. The answer was surprisingly simple. He wrote a code onto each shoebox when he received them from his vendor. He used the local city in North Carolina, Rockingham, as the code. Rockingham has ten digits, and he used a substitution code to write letters representing the price onto each box. Therefore, he would write "CR.MM" on the box, and this meant "$20.99" as his cost. At a glance, he knew what he had paid and was able to quickly mark down the prices or offer bulk savings on sales as he saw fit and still made a profit. An old-fashioned approach fit the situation to a tee.

Don't Ignore Old Methods

We were at the end of a long six weeks of work preparing our financial statements for the first time as a newly divested company. The company was also subject to fast approaching Securities and Exchange Commission (SEC) filing deadlines. After a long six weeks in which I was drafted into an interim position backfilling the controller and dealing with late nights, auditors, a physical location move, and launching our own financial systems, the deadline was looming, and we were almost there. That is, until the new system would not produce the automated cash flow statement as required.

It was the night before the filing deadline and the day before I was scheduled to take the family on a Thanksgiving trip to see my parents in Texas. In other words, we were flying at full speed to cross the finish line at the last minute. This wasn't terribly shocking given the challenges we faced, but the finish line was in sight. Then, the cash flow report issue occurred. The team, most of them ten years or more younger than me, stood around at about 8:00 p.m. in utter disbelief and defeat. You could see in their eyes there was no way to solve the problem, and we would be subject to fines and embarrassment at missing our first filing deadline as a new company. It was then that I told the team to print out the financial statements, grab a calculator and some paper, and meet me in the new CFO's office with a cup of coffee.

The new CFO hadn't even joined the company yet, and the old one had stopped showing up at the office. Despite the lack of leadership, it did give me a big, empty table to work at. The team showed up with the supplies and information but questioned what I was doing. When I told them that I would build the cash flow statement by hand, they replied "That's impossible!" You see, being a bit younger, they had not experienced a time when you had to do things the old-fashioned way. It was so far from their thinking; they saw it as impossible.

Three and a half hours and several cups of coffee later, we had a cash flow statement and had completed the work for filing on time. The team learned the impossible was possible, and when we fixed the computer issues, we discovered the automated report was a near-match for what we had done the "old-fashioned way".

Get the Shelves out of the Basement

We were moving into a newly purchased used house, and the previous owner had been nice enough to leave some furniture in the basement. We quickly discovered her kindness was likely more related to the furniture being heavy or awkward to get out of the basement. While we moved things into the house, we asked our daughter's friends to move the stuff out of the basement and into the garage so we could determine what we wanted to keep.

They successfully wrestled the very heavy sleeper sofa and recliner up the back stairs but not without a fair amount of pain and muscle exhaustion. Therefore, I was surprised when they went quiet for a while, and we didn't see the metal bookcases come upstairs. After about 30 minutes, they came upstairs and stated, "We can't figure out how they got these shelves in the basement! And we can't get them upstairs." I went downstairs, and the metal shelves were in a different room and much farther from the stairs than when they started. To me, the solution was simple: unbolt the four bolts holding the two bookshelves together and move them up one at a time. To the guys, it hadn't even crossed their mind to take a different approach. In this case, my experience and old-school solution worked and the solved problem in five minutes.

Using Flint and Steel

In a world where new technology is everywhere and the computing power in our cell phones is more than the computer that launched astronauts to the moon, what can be learned from these examples, and more importantly, how do you balance embracing new technology with holding onto the ability to function in an old-fashioned manner when the technology fails? Flint and steel can light a fire just as a lighter with lighter fluid. What are some approaches you can take?

1. Learn the fundamentals. Just because the computer automatically does something, doesn't mean you shouldn't learn the basics. Even spellcheck can't fix your spelling errors 100% of the time if you have zero idea how to spell. You should also learn how to type efficiently. Yes, hunting and pecking works, but it costs a lot of time compared to learning the proper method. Learning the basics here can save a lot of time and errors and the time it takes correcting those errors.
2. Stay in touch with the basics. Yes, you can and should use the time-saving tools and technologies available. However, it shouldn't stop you from using basic processes from time to time. Make it a game. Can you beat the computer, or in the example before, are you as accurate as the computer program?

3. Learn the *how* behind the technology. Can you explain the technology to your grandparents? If not, you may be viewing it as a magic box that produces work rather than as a tool to assist you.
4. Test the technology. Can you break it? How reliable is it? This avoids the magic box approach. The truth is, most modern computer systems are very good although not truly automatic like major home appliances. When you start your oven, it works. It doesn't give you warning errors or cook your food at the completely wrong temperature.

DON'T FALL FOR THE CHAFF

"Blowing Chaff" is a term used by the Air Force as a technique to get the enemy's radar to lock onto a cloud of aluminum strips rather than the aircraft.[27] Basically, when the aircraft has been spotted and the radar is about to pick them up to allow a missile to strike them, they *blow chaff* out of the jet and make a radical turn in the other direction. The missile then locks onto the radar and strikes the cloud of aluminum strips, allowing the jet to escape.

In The Band's classic song "The Weight," the main character takes a trip and is continually faced with situations and characters who distract him from his goal. These include

- A stranger refused to offer him ideas for a place to stay
- Carmen wants to stick him with the Devil
- Luke wants him to keep Anna Lee company
- Crazy Chester wants him to watch and feed his dog[28]

Basically, he keeps on taking the load from others and only late in the song realizes he needs to get back to Fanny who sent him there just to say hello to everyone. In this admittedly literal translation of the song, he is continually distracted by *chaff* from his mission. Do you find yourself distracted by *chaff* in the workplace?

$49,900 in the Suitcase

I had a very simple task—or so I thought. My job was to collect the fees for new franchisees on the first day of training. I tried not to be too aggressive, as people usually walked in with their checks and gave them to me. My practice was to wait until the lunch break and then pay the folks who hadn't paid a visit.

One individual was a new franchisee from South America who had made his money in the jewel business. *What in the world did that mean?* He hadn't paid, and lunch time had arrived. I quietly pulled him aside, and he said, "Let me go outside and get my suitcase."

This prompted me to ask him, "So, your checkbook is in your suitcase?"

He replied, "No, the cash is in the suitcase."

Visions of every stereotype of South America ran through my head. What exactly was the jewel business? Was it code for more illicit substances? What would happen to me if I took in nearly $50,000 in cash? Was it money laundering? In his way, the franchisee was *blowing chaff* by distracting me from worrying about the implications of accepting the cash because by doing so, I could follow the rules and collect the required amount on day one of training. This was also the only way the company got to count it as revenue.

After a minute of contemplation, I responded with a list of local banks and told him he needed to go deposit the contents of the unseen suitcase. I didn't want to see the suitcase or even want it in the building. He could bring a certified check the next day to me. I reported the situation to my boss and determined that if he didn't show up with the funds, we could remove him from training on day two if necessary. He showed up with the check, and it all turned out ok after I avoided the *chaff*.

Rock Collections and M&Ms

Not everyone at this client was on board with consultants helping them find ways to improve. In fact, the very successful client had team members willing to distract both of us, as consultants, and their own team through building a rock museum and feeding them M&Ms for free in every break room that served as their own form of *chaff*.

The rock collection had absolutely nothing to do with the business of the company. However, the owner built massive displays in buildings on campus to show off his collection. Employees would be encouraged to view them, and they even took us as consultants to see the rocks. I have nothing against rocks, but they had nothing to do with our project. They were *chaff* to distract us from the task at hand.

The cafeterias. Yes, there were numerous cafeterias, and they were more of the same type of distractions. Without a doubt, the best employee cafeteria food I'd ever seen at about one-third of the market price. They had omelets, sushi, quiche, custom entrees—almost anything you could imagine. Did it have anything to do with the mission of the company? Absolutely nothing. It provided, at a fairly high cost, a distraction for the employees from the challenges of the company with declining profits.

Last was the collection of free snacks, including M&Ms, both peanut and plain, in every breakroom on every floor of every building. This was a benefit to the employees, but the amount of time they spent eating M&Ms and gathering together talking, rather than working, was unbelievable. It had grown over time, and no one really saw the cost both in food supplies and in wasted time. It got so bad that I responded to the client when I realized they were building another multi-story office building they didn't need. I told them that if they weren't willing to cut staff to a reasonable level, they could at least remove them from work duties and put them in the empty building and feed them M&Ms. It would at least allow them to streamline their processes. My message at least got partially through. Several years later, the team now refers to the new building as the M&M Building. It was *chaff* to distract us and their employees from the real issues the organization needed to face.

Arm Wrestling over a Simple Agreement

Working with a university a few years ago, one of our tasks was to achieve agreement between individuals operating different organizations on one way of operating with each other, including escalating issues and interacting with a third-party vendor. As this was a key task we were being paid for, we dedicated our time to working through this.

The different organizations were not at all in favor of working together. They started fights and figuratively arm-wrestled over every word in our draft agreement. We offered multiple drafts, and we even offered to implement their proposed revisions. Then, they started arguing over the whole concept but wouldn't offer direct feedback. I'm sorry to admit, but for a good amount of time, I fell for the *chaff* and spent a lot of time revising documents and holding meetings with different leaders to get them on board. Hours upon wasted hours for zero results and angry project stakeholders.

Oddly enough, their final action is what removed the *chaff* and allowed us to move forward. They got together to write, and each signed, a letter to their senior management objecting to the whole concept. Senior management agreed, and this stopped the activity, relieving us of our assigned task. This freed us to focus only on the organizations who wanted to participate. Once we eliminated the distractions, we accomplished our objectives much more rapidly and focused on the core tasks at hand.

How to Ignore the *Chaff*

Chaff is probably more common in organizations than it is in the military. Just as fighters need to realize when someone is blowing *chaff*, you need to keep your eyes for the same in your organization. How do you avoid having "the load" put on you, as the song says? The load isn't yours to carry and is likely *chaff*. The following steps will help you do this:

1. Think about what is happening. If someone brings up an extraneous detail or something else while you are working on a key objective, make sure you recognize this is happening.
2. Write it down. Document what they are saying.
3. Stay on task. It is fine to say, "Thanks for sharing," or "That's an interesting point—can we talk about that next week?" In fact, this is far more effective than following the distraction and missing a deadline or objective.
4. Recognize when you are falling for the *chaff*. Turn the situation back around and refocus your attention on important matters.
5. Recognize when you may do the same. It is something all of us can find ourselves doing, especially when things aren't going well. Don't tolerate the behavior in yourself.

RECOVERING FROM THE IRRECOVERABLE SPIN

The Beatles had a song on *Sergeant Pepper's Lonely Hearts Club Band* called "Getting Better" that contrasts getting better in a situation because it seems things can't get worse.[29]

Yes, sometimes things go bad, and you feel like they can't get worse. Sometimes, you are the cause of it going bad. However, more importantly than not ever making mistakes, which is impossible, is having an ability to recover from your mistakes and get back on the right track. It's even better if your recovery behavior puts you in a better place than before. It can get better when "it can't get no worse."

The Elevator Ate My Keys

I was a newly responsible student manager at the campus food service my freshman year in college. Yes, I took the job, because otherwise, I would be stuck being a dishwasher, soaking wet and miserable in front of my new college friends and classmates. Yes, I let the "manager" in the title go to my head a little bit. I was due to be humbled.

Everyone had left the cafeteria on Friday night, and it was my responsibility to lock up the building. Riding the elevator down from the second floor, I brushed the doorframe and my keys, which were hanging out of my back pocket, fell out. *No big deal*, I thought. *I'll just pick them up.* It turns out it wasn't very easy.

The keys had fallen through the gap between the elevator and the main floor down below the elevator in an inaccessible area four feet away. The gap was too narrow to reach my hand through. I called campus security, and they didn't have the keys to lock up. That was a weird response from security, but perhaps they just didn't want to be bothered. Additionally, the keys to my dorm and car were on the same keyring. I next tried the elevator company, and they did not offer after-hours service. They were going to make me wait for them to come out Monday morning. *Ugh!* As a new manager, I didn't want to call my boss and let him know of my carelessness. Eventually, I devised a method using a long broomstick and an unfolded metal coat hanger that I duct-taped to the broomstick. I fished the keys out after about two hours of trying, then I locked up the building, and my recovery strategy became putting my keys completely in my pocket which I haven't forgotten since that moment.

The Old Gas Stove

Well, I needed a haircut, and it was time to shave my beard anyway! That's what I told myself on Saturday morning. I woke up early, took a shower, and rode my bike across town, frustrated that the VW Bug was once again not working, and I didn't have the money to fix it. Then, I walked into the diner in which I was the assistant manager. (As a side note, watch out. These titles are typically handed out when you are a mixture of cook and dishwasher, and they give you these titles to make you feel better. It did, however, look better on my resume.) I proceeded with my first job to light the 1940s gas grill. I turned on the main gas from about 15 feet away, walked to the stove, lit the match, and was reaching for the gas control on the grill. *Ka-blam!* Orange and blue fire shot out of the grill, blowing me backward into the counter. The owner was sitting at the table and looked at me as if he were seeing a ghost when I slowly stood up.

Apparently, the previous night's closing staff had taken a shortcut and not shut off the gas at the grill. This allowed the gas to build up when I walked from the main line to the grill. When I lit the match, I was treated to a few burns on my left hand, all the hair burned off from the left arm, my beard singed on the left side of my face, and burns on my forehead. Thankfully, my stylish, oversized 1980s glasses saved my eyes. My hair burned to a frizzy crisp all the way around the left side of my head.

My recovery strategy? I went next door to the pharmacy and bought some burn ointment and a comb. After a quick trip to the restroom to comb off the frizzy hair and apply burn ointment, I relit the gas grill and worked the shift. I looked really odd with a half-burned-off beard but proved to the owner, who must have been thinking he was about to be sued, I would see it through despite a rough start. The shower and bike ride in the mist turned out to have helped save me from worse injuries as the moisture kept me from a worse outcome!

Go Call the Police—I'll Stall Them!

There came a day that I learned four people attacking you at once really isn't as bad as it sounds. They really do get in their own way, which keeps them from all hitting you at once. It was my second day on the job as the manager of a repossessed apartment complex on the edge of the bad side of town. I'd lived there a year, and after multiple managers left, I approached the management company when they were visiting to tell them this was an issue, and "I could do a better job" managing the complex. My thinking was "it can't get no worse," as the song said. It should have been a sign when they immediately gave the job to a 20-year-old college student. For me, it was a work from home situation with part-time hours, a free apartment, utilities, cable, and a whopping $250 a month!

The second day on the job, we returned from watching a movie and noticed four young men who didn't live in the complex surrounding our neighbor, Mrs. Pritchard. Mrs. Pritchard was about 80 years old and not in the best shape to defend herself. I told my wife to go call the police, and I'd talk to them to defuse the situation. When I walked down the sidewalk, I learned people are not always interested in a conversation. The good news is, I distracted them from Mrs. Pritchard. The bad news was the leader of the group immediately threw a punch with brass knuckles on his hand, which broke my nose and knocked me to the ground. They then took turns kicking and punching me. Somehow in the melee, I got hold of the leader, and using my best 8th grade wrestling moves, I managed to get him in a headlock and started pounding his head on the concrete. I picked him up and thought I had the upper hand; however, he pulled a knife and held it up against my side. *Ok, so it could get worse*, I thought after the fact. As the police were entering the complex, I let him go. They chased them down, and according to the arresting officer, they were going to throw them in the holding cell with a couple of guys on PCP. With the adrenaline surging and my body covered head to toe with blood, I turned to the onlookers raging about this being the reason we needed to improve the complex into a better place to live. I'm sure I was quite the sight to see.

After a quick trip to the emergency room in which the doctor stitched me up and said that although I had a broken nose, I either had "a very hard head, or they had soft shoes." He then sent me home.

My dad and mom had arrived. Dad brought me an axe handle. He advised, "It's better than a baseball bat because no one is going to confuse what you intend to do with the axe handle." Armed with both the knowledge and the axe handle, I was back on the job the next day, patrolling the complex. Between the fear of my raging the night before and the fact I was walking around with an axe handle looking like the living dead, the complex improved very rapidly. In fact, six months later, we were awarded the "Most Improved" award for all of the properties in the Greater Austin area. We made a complex on the decline a little better.

Don't Forget to Breathe!

I got the call in the backseat of a cab in Toronto while I was riding with our CFO back to the airport. We were in days before our year-end close, and the accounting system had died. This was a serious issue a colleague and I had worried about for over a year, and it came at the worst possible time. The company was quickly going into a tailspin from which we might not recover.

The controller and I had asked for a new system for over a year as the system we had was antiquated, and we had grown from a $200 million company to $1 billion in sales in about two years. The system was held together with duct tape and bailing wire and felt like it was always about to fail. However, the requests had been turned down by the CFO. This was due first to the expense, and second, a different division had recently spent millions of dollars on a failed software implementation. Yet here I was dealing with the controller on his honeymoon sailing in the Caribbean and the CFO and I in a different country.

"Will it print the files?" I asked the supervisor. "Ok, then print the files for each location, gather the administrative assistants, and fax each of the files to the locations." That way, the locations could at least review the files and determine what they needed to do to close the books. This was 1998, and faxes were not used like that. You sent data files via email, but the option was not possible. I would buy the time to get back to Houston. The CFO, hearing only my side of the conversation, had a puzzled look on his face. I explained the system failure to him, doing my best to not say "I told you so," and before we reached the airport, he approved buying a new computer system.

Arriving in Houston, we were able to put another piece of virtual duct tape on the system and get it temporarily functioning. After six months of hard work (and crossing our fingers the old system would hold together), we had a new system in place for the division that became the model for the rest of the company. We not only recovered by fixing the immediate problem but emerged in a better situation.

The Worst Conference Call in the History of the Universe

We had worked on winning the work from the client for four years, and I saw it going down in flames! Early in the stages of working with the client, we were holding a global conference call with all of their finance staff with more than two hundred people in attendance. We deferred, as we usually did at the time, to the client, and they wanted to use their teleconference system. That decision turned out to be a big mistake.

It was a brief 30-minute call walking the team through a basic information gathering exercise and the spreadsheet template. However, it immediately took a wrong turn when people started joining the call. "*Beep*—Joe Smith has joined the call. *Beep*—Sally Johnson has joined the call." On and on it went for the first 15 minutes of the call, constantly interrupting me as I walked everyone through the basic information. I signaled to another co-worker to have our IT person change the notifications, but as it wasn't our system, he couldn't fix the problem. We had about five minutes of silence from the incessant beeping, and then at 20 minutes into the call, people began to disconnect. I didn't really blame them, but the beeping and "Joe Smith has left the call" began for the final ten minutes of the call. I ended the call, and we all just sat in the room defeated. It felt like the worst conference call in the history of the universe. After a few minutes, I knew I had to do something but wasn't quite sure what to do.

I was reminded of another time when I made a bad decision and got involved in April Fool's Day pranks in junior high. Facing the consequences, my dad insisted I own up immediately to the problem to deal with it and the suspension I received. With that in mind, I went down the client's hallway to confess to the problem that had happened. I proposed holding another call on another teleconference system the next day. It gave us about a 10% chance, at best, of retaining the client. I walked down the hall wondering if they would even pay for our flights back from London to the U.S. However, they appreciated me owning the issue and coming up with a recovery plan that made sense. We moved on from the bad call to another 18 months of work with the client and exited with a successful project behind us.

Pulling up to Better Results

There are a number of ways to develop a recovery strategy and make things better in bad situations. Some of them, you can actually plan in advance, and some require more practice at improvisation. A few ways that can help are as follows:

1. Plan ideas, options, and plan B (or C, D, and E) before entering into a situation. Brainstorm what you are going to do if something goes wrong.
2. Remember to breathe. We would have had disaster if I didn't see the call through and if I didn't spend a few minutes brainstorming how to fix the situation.
3. Own it. Do not put the blame on anyone else. It's not acceptable to blame others for your situation and play the victim. This is not a good leadership approach and does not lead to others respecting your abilities.
4. Fix it. Find a way to not only recover but end up with better results through your recovery. In the case with our client, we gained respect for the organization which led to a good long-term engagement. In the case of the apartment complex, not only did my

wounds heal and the culprits go to jail, but we also made the apartment complex a better place to live.

Always look for a way to be "Getting Better" on a daily basis in work.

FINDING GOOD IN BAD SITUATIONS

It's appropriate for a song performed by David Allan Coe to open this chapter. In "You Never Even Call Me by My Name," he sang about staying the course through bad situations.[30]

This is a great example of being in a bad situation but being determined to see it through and making the best of what is occurring.

The Best Half-Concert Ever

As the lights went up and the police and police dogs came into the Moose Lodge, huffing and puffing, Catherine and I turned to each other and decided it might be time to leave. We didn't know exactly how the situation reached this level so quickly, but we could agree it was time to get out of Dodge!

Finding Good in Bad Situations

It all started with me rediscovering outlaw country music on Pandora radio, eventually leading back from Johnny Cash, Willie Nelson, Waylon Jennings, and Merle Haggard to David Allan Coe. There's spending some time in jail and calling yourself an outlaw, and then there is spending from nine years old to 29 in Starr Reform School and at least three years in the Ohio Penitentiary. Coe wasn't fooling when he wrote "Death Row." He truly lived the outlaw country life he sang about. In fact, when he moved to Nashville, he supposedly lived out of a hearse that he parked in front of the Ryman Auditorium while looking for a record deal.

When the opportunity came to see him live in person, we were sold. Though, it was a bit strange as famous as he was for him to be performing at the local Moose Lodge.

We parked at the bottom of the hill, hiked up to the Lodge, and joined the crowd drinking beer. Finding folding seats lined up in the room was a bit of a shock, but then again, we knew we weren't at a concert hall. We were about five rows back. After several rounds of the crowd drinking,

Coe and the band performed, and the crowd stood up and filled the space in front of the stage. Several songs in, all 5-feet-2-inches of Catherine decided to weave through the crowd to get all the way to the front to take some pictures.

Just about the time she snuck back through the crowd to her seat, the Moose Lodge security interrupted the concert and announced, "Y'all are violating fire codes! If you don't back up from the stage and go back to your seats, we will stop the concert again!" There was a resounding lack of reaction as no one moved back or sat down. Catherine and I looked at each other. At that moment, I was glad she was back from her adventure at the stage. About that time, Coe's wife and back-up singer spoke into the microphone: "Y'all need to back up and sit down, or I swear to God, I'll take my husband and the band, and we will pack up and be gone!" Again, this was followed by a non-reaction.

Crash! Someone started throwing punches, then the beer started flying, and folding chairs were being used as weapons. Chaos quickly ensued, and we were only one row away from the melee. The lights went up, and when we looked at the stage after what I swear felt like only one minute, the entire band was gone. Catherine and I stood there with the rest of the crowd wondering if they were going to come back. The police and their dogs showed up out of breath from having to park at the base of the hill and run up. We looked at each other and took that as our cue to exit. As we crossed paths with other angry officers and dogs, we counted 20 police cars as we migrated to our car. We also saw the band's bus pull out of the parking lot. Laughing and sharing our thoughts about our favorite songs, we made the best of the situation. We didn't get the full concert, but we get one hell of an experience and the best half-concert we've ever seen!

Miami Vice Was a Long Time Ago

I found myself wondering how I became *the guy* to go to places no one wanted to visit. Perhaps I should have avoided finding a way to Sri Lanka after all! I was sitting in the Mexico City Airport for several hours waiting for my flight to Colombia. Visions of drug cartels and the *Miami Vice* television show replayed themselves in my head. Did they really need me to go for the meeting with the potential client? Would the phone please ring and tell me they cancelled the meeting? What was wrong with video-conferencing? Why did I learn basic, very basic Spanish? I'm open to visiting most places but didn't want to go there at all. Not one iota.

Despite my desires, the cancellation phone call didn't come, and I reluctantly got on the plane. I was pleasantly surprised it wasn't the *Miami Vice* 1985 in Colombia. Although there are rougher areas, the environment was safe and people very friendly. In fact, I met one of our Latin American consultants who was from Colombia on the trip. He has since worked with me on several North American projects and became a key support and friend to me over the last several years with projects in the U.S., Canada, and Europe.

I found with each of these examples that by facing your fears, good things came out of the experience. During my trip, I fulfilled company obligations, met new people, expanded our business, and built a business relationship and friendship that has been fantastic over the years. It is hard to imagine what I would have missed out on if I let fear sit in the driver's seat. Good definitely came out of looking beyond what I initially perceived to be a bad situation.

The Great Escape

Steve McQueen looked pretty fricking cool running from the Nazis and trying to jump a fence with a motorcycle to finalize his escape from the POW camp. And the movie was based on a true story! I've since learned it doesn't mean much as the movie industry does stretch the *true* in "true story." The older man standing in 1985 before my 11th grade history class in Ozark, Alabama, didn't look or act like Steve McQueen, but his story was fascinating. Jerry Sage was a retired Colonel who had served in the OSS in World War II and was captured and held by the Nazis in a POW camp. Elements of his story were the true foundation of *The Great Escape*.

Yet here he was, talking of risks far greater than any shown in the movie. Yes, he was the man in charge of hiding over 200,000 pounds of sand from the three-tunnel escape route. The movie made it almost look like a fun time. In reality, he had to dispose of his OSS gear, pretend to be a downed pilot, and endure torture. Had it been discovered he was an OSS agent; he would have been immediately executed as a spy. However, this didn't stop him from teaching other prisoners his silent killing technique. He, in keeping with his motivation and training, found a way to keep driving toward the goals of the Allies. He found good in a bad situation.[31] Through Colonel Sage's account, I began to understand why my grandfather, himself a POW in World War II, couldn't stand the *Hogan's Heroes* comedy about a POW camp. No movie or TV show could convey the level of risk these veterans took.

This encouraged me to learn more about my grandfather's experiences in World War II. He rarely spoke about his time in the war other than being frustrated when *Hogan's Heroes* was on television. Frustrated with his father's insistence on him pursuing an engineering degree, he had signed a 20-year enlistment. (Yes, they had 20-year enlistments in those days.) He joined the Army Air Corps. In the 1940s, his plane was shot down. As he used to say, he was going to land his parachute safely until it came down to choosing between an apple tree or a brick wall. Actually, he avoided the apple tree and crashed into the brick wall shattering one of his legs. Soon, he was captured and made a prisoner of war. His first opportunity to make the best of the situation was when his doctor told him he had been experimenting with wiring shattered bones back together. He offered to do this for my grandfather. My grandfather, in pain and concerned, asked about the risks. He was told if it didn't work, he would walk with a limp for the rest of his life.

"And if we don't wire the bone together?" my grandfather asked.

"Then, you will definitely walk with a limp for the rest of your life" was the response.

My grandfather made the best of a bad decision and, for the rest of his life, had zero problem with the leg once it had healed. Being a POW was a bit touchier for him as he was the son of a recent German immigrant to the U.S. and could speak and read German fluently. If this were discovered, he would have been perceived as a traitor and likely executed. Despite not being able to escape due to his injury, he still found good for the other POWs in a bad situation.

He decided to play crazy with the Germans. He would puzzlingly look at their newspapers upside down and ball them up for insulation under his coat. Hobbling back to his quarters, he would then extract them and translate them for the rest of the prisoners—giving them insights into what was going on in the war. He grew out a goatee and let his hair get long, and with his dark complexion, which was ironically from his German roots, he convinced them he was a crazy Indian chief from America.

Robert's grandfather as a POW in World War II

It was like a magic trick or confidence game, but it held serious consequences if he was discovered. After his leg healed, his captors knew he still couldn't run far, so he was tasked with going to the local fields to gather vegetables for the guards. In his coat pockets, he would hide potatoes and other vegetables. Upon return to camp, when asked if he had anything in his pockets, he would tell them directly, "I have two potatoes in this pocket and onions and carrots in the others." With the reputation for being crazy, they would laugh and let him into the camp where he could help feed the other prisoners. He gained his freedom in May 1945 and was soon back in the U.S. As an ironic ending to this time, he learned he had enough points to leave the military due to his service and time in the POW camp. He refused this early departure, because as he said, "I signed up for 20 years, and that was my promise." His evaluators thought he truly was crazy not to leave. After a quick side-trip for a psychological evaluation in which he was found sane, he not only served out his 20 years but tacked on ten more to the end of his career.

Sometimes, movies make things look more exciting than real life. However, the examples of Colonel Sage and my grandfather are good to demonstrate how to make the best of bad situations.

The Art of Truck Tackling

I woke to the unmistakable sound of a Volkswagen Bug horn being blown multiple times. As my wife and I had the only VW at the apartments, I had a pretty good idea it was her. I went out the back of the apartment to the parking lot to see what was going on. She was circling in and out of the parking lot from one entrance to an exit and back again, all while honking the horn. A guy in a dark blue pickup truck was following her. Round and round they went, with no sign of stopping. I stood there trying figure out how to get this very bad situation solved for the best.

It seemed a bad idea to go back in and call the police and wait. In my view, nothing was going to be gained, and with each second, the risk of someone wrecking or worse increased. It dawned on me what I had to do, and I jumped into action.

I realized the truck driver had to slow down a bit to enter the parking lot, and I made a beeline for the truck, grabbing the door handle and the front of the bed. It stopped him. Have you heard those stories of people lifting cars after a wreck due to adrenaline? This isn't one of those stories. I didn't develop some sort of super-strength. Rather, I shocked the truck driver when he found himself dragging a total stranger across a parking lot. Beyond stopping him, it did allow my wife to park her car and get into the apartment in safety. I let go of the truck, and he skidded to a stop. Imagine my surprise when he got out of the truck, and he looked, at first glance, to be wearing a police uniform!

Looking more closely, it was a security guard uniform, but he was armed with a pistol. He started to reach for the gun, all while swearing a blue streak. I realized I had to figure out how to make the best of this increasingly bad situation. *Should I turn and run for cover?* No, doing that would just make my back a target for this crazy man. Instead, I rapidly closed the distance between us and dared him to draw. I told him, "Go ahead and draw the gun. There is no way this ends well for you!" at the distance of about two feet. His bluster faded off, and thankfully, he didn't draw. He tried to say it was my wife's fault, and I told him to get in his truck and leave, or I'd call the police, and we'd let them sort it out. He rapidly drove off and left us behind.

Apparently, my wife, in her desire to get home from a long day at work, had cut him off on the highway, and he didn't like it. She was running out of gas, which is why she chose to come home rather than drive several miles farther to the police station. We never heard another peep out of him, and by ending the very bad situation, we made the best of it.

Escaping the Maze

We all find ourselves in bad situations. Some are temporary and minor, some absolutely life-threatening. In bad situations, like in our David Allan Coe song of "standing in the rain" and waiting, we have to endure and make the best of it. Here are some tips for making the best of a bad situation:

1. Pause and look around. Get your bearings and determine where you are.
2. Understand the risks around you.
3. Develop the action plan and approach to make the best of the situation.

RISE MORE RAPIDLY

Following are some ideas on how to draw attention to yourself (in a good way) and increase your chances of getting promoted.

I was very excited to finally have the new job—and entering a two-week onboarding period prior to the official three-week training program. I was joined by one other trainee, Harry, who was a few years older than me. We were given clear objectives and steps we were supposed to take. Most of it was pretty boring training sessions on basic software while sitting at a computer. However, these were tools in which we needed proven competency, so I followed the checklist and did the work. Meanwhile, Harry was almost never in the training room. He walked around headquarters, meeting people, shaking hands, joking, and going to lunch with new team members. Meanwhile, there I sat following the checklists as required.

There was another trainee in the room, Bob Smith, who had been with the company for a couple of months. I was surprised when he turned to me on day three and said, "Well, I can see you won't be a superstar like Harry, but you will probably be a very good worker bee." He went on to describe how Harry was going to get promoted due to his superior social skills and ways with people, but people like me have their places in organizations too.

I didn't respond, but it definitely left me wondering. Since when was a new employee following what they were told to do in their first week at a new job a bad thing? How did he know what my future, or Harry's, was in the company? Was I supposed to ignore the direction I was given? I was both confused and irritated. Still irritated enough six weeks later, when offered me the opportunity to help a failing manager in Austin, I turned the opportunity down. Rather, I offered to take over management of the store, cutting my 18 months of planned training into two months. If the existing manager had driven the store into the ground in six months, I couldn't help him. The response was "well, you'd have to fire him then." So, I drove to Austin, fired the poorly performing manager, and truly began my career in turning around a location. By the way, upon returning to headquarters in about a year and a half, I discovered Harry had never done any actual work and had some sort of meltdown that resulted in his rapid exit from the organization. So much for labeling people "rock stars" and "worker bees" in week one.

BUY THE UTENSILS

Billy Joel had a song called "I Go to Extremes" with lyrics about feeling on the top of the world.[32]

Although it also talks about the feelings at the other extreme, these lyrics represent overachieving to me and taking your shot when you get the chance.

The Admin Assistant as HR Head?

After a couple of years of near-constant employee reductions and restructuring, the company was about one-third the size it had been before. It was smaller, and somehow, Sally, the administrative assistant to the CEO, had been given the additional duties of human resources, as well as serving as the Office Manager. She quickly proved through her actions she had no experience in these areas. She had, in a sense, overachieved, and her actions were proving this to the entire company.

One of her major actions was to remove the plastic silverware from the employee breakroom to reduce costs.

Our location was about 15 minutes away from any restaurants, and having the plasticware available was a way to keep the employees onsite. This allowed them to get quickly back to their desks. The cost of employees being offsite cost far more than the cost of plastic knives, forks, and spoons. I even asked her about it, and she bragged about how much money she was saving the company. All the while, I saw them wheel meals, literally on silver trays, from the cafeteria to the new CEO's office. Having his meals produced and delivered daily was undoubtedly more expensive than plastic utensils.

However, you have to determine the extent of your influence, and arguing about the CEO's lunch delivery was going to get me nowhere and fast. However, a quick trip the supermarket during my lunch hour combined with some quick calculations led me to an action I could take. I returned to the office with six months of plasticware and put it in the breakroom. Sally caught me doing this and wanted to know what I was up to. I told her I'd just bought six months' worth of plasticware for $30 and was donating them to the team. Because I continued to do this, I had more influence on reducing costs than anything Sally had accomplished. This overachievement from what was in my job description brought positive reactions from the rest of the team.

Sicker than a Dog in Iowa

One of my key project leaders was sick in her hotel room. She had gotten sick in route from London to Iowa. We were in the final week of the on-site work with our client. Desperate for a solution, I brought soup to her hotel room. Soup fixes everything, right? However, they didn't have chicken broth, and I didn't think things through. I ended up bringing some type of corn chowder, and the smell alone sent her running to the bathroom. I didn't help a bit; I made it worse.

I made it so much worse that another key leader had to drive her to urgent care at the same time that we had two major events occurring. Now I wasn't down one person but two. I was left with only two fairly new employees, where I needed two for each event. My only choice was to fill in on one of the events myself, diving in the details. I chose to pair up with the newest, and less experienced, employee, while the only thing I could tell the other guy was "someone may be able to join you mid-way … just do your best".

We managed to recover from the situation and find our way through the events without causing issues for our client. My sick project leader got some medicine and traveled back to London to recover to work on a number of other projects. In this case, the recovery wasn't visible to the client, which is even better from my perspective. The *new guy* who I left on his own has also gone on to become a successful project manager.

Why Did I Take This Job?

It had seemed like a good idea to move to the new job. Same title, bigger organization, higher pay, and the same commute time. Why wouldn't I take the job? Seemed like a no-brainer at the time. Surely, this wouldn't turn into a bad situation.

Well, I joined on the first day of the year-end close for a company that had only recently made two major acquisitions, removed their resources doing the corporate accounting, and were going through a major financial system conversion. Every single day for the first several weeks was a nightmare. Every day, I went home questioning my decision to take the job. I wondered if my old company would take me back or if I should start looking for a new job. The low point happened when I, along with three other colleagues, were tasked with making a $25 million reduction to our worldwide bonus accrual. It was late at night on day nine of the close, and we were tired and a little fuzzy, which is why there were four of involved rather than one or two. I keyed the entries while the others looked over my shoulders. Fairly quickly, we finished the transaction and gave the word the results could be loaded into our consolidating financial system. This would take overnight to process, so we could go home. We arrived back the next morning feeling relaxed and a bit accomplished. Getting a call from the controller, Jim, was a surprise. Laughing, he said, "Were you guys tired last night?"

I replied, "A little bit." He laughed again and said, "Why don't you guys check the financial statements and give me a call back in a few minutes?" We did and were horrified to find the profit for the company was $50 million worse than we had calculated the night before. A quick check showed we had booked the entry completely backwards even with four sets of eyes on it. We called the controller back, and he just said, "Fix it now," and we did. No further repercussions were felt except to increase my thoughts I had picked the wrong place to work.

Nevertheless, I chose to stick it out and find a way to make good out of the bad situation and embarrassment. By the end of three months, it was a great job, and my team was producing good results, and I received a promotion after nine months.

Overachievement Is OK

There are many different ways to get promoted more rapidly. Are you "clear as a crystal and sharp as a knife," as the song says? If not, what can you do to move in a direction toward overachievement in your role? The following are some ways to start down the road to overachievement:

1. Put in the time. Some say if you put in 10,000 hours into something, you can become a world expert. This equates to only five years of full-time employment. Don't expect instantaneous expertise.
2. Work for more knowledge. Have you checked books out on your areas of interest and actually read them? What about knowledge in areas you aren't involved in? Are you learning about the core responsibilities in your business? Even if you are in IT, for example, it helps if you learn about your company's core industry.
3. Join an organization or attend conferences. This is another way of networking and gaining knowledge.
4. Train others on a topic. Often, the act of preparing and delivering training to other people forces you to understand the topic better. Additionally, being a trainer on a topic increases the positive perception others have of you.
5. Find a mentor. Who is the expert in your company? Who is the expert outside of your company? People are often surprised by how open leaders are to helping others new in their field or industry.
6. Ask questions. You don't have to know it all. Ask questions and look for different ways to approach a situation. It might be as simple as buying some plastic utensils, but you will be rightly perceived as a problem-solver in your organization.
7. Take on the nastiest projects. It is rare to get a rapid promotion by just doing the work in the job

description. Volunteer to take on the project in trouble or on fire. If you fail to turn it around, it won't look bad as if the managers already saw it as a disaster. However, when you fix it and turn it around, you will be seen as a hero. Either way, you were willing to put yourself into an uncomfortable situation, and this behavior will serve you well in the future.

8. Realize you will have bad days. You may even have bad weeks or months. Pick yourself up and keep moving forward.

KEEP GOING IF YOU KNOW YOU'RE RIGHT

There's a great example in the Wings hit "Live and Let Die" with lyrics that talk about doing the job you were hired to do and doing it well.[33]

There's a time and a place when they wouldn't have hired you if they didn't need the help. You are there for a reason and need to see things through and use your expertise.

Ignore the Experts (Sometimes)

I was getting my feet under me for about a year into my new job and found something that looked really odd. My job was to do the accounting, but if I found something wrong, my instincts were to latch onto it like a dog to a bone to get it fixed. My goal with this book isn't to provide an accounting education, but basically, you collect sales tax when you sell a product and then turn around and give it to the state. This doesn't change your revenue as your company doesn't get to keep the money. You just hold this 7% temporarily for a few days and give it over to the states. Well, I was looking at our numbers and discovered our accrual, where we were holding the money temporarily for the states, was growing at an unbelievable rate while our sales numbers had been dropping. It didn't make any sense. I talked to the tax people in a different department responsible for giving the money to the states and was told they were sending the money monthly, and all was well.

I was stopped cold for a moment. However, I spent some evening and weekend time looking through the transactions, and they weren't making any sense at all. I went to my boss and subsequently to his boss to talk about the issue. My bosses' boss said, "If you know you are right, just keep going. Let's see where this leads. I'll tell the tax department you are continuing to double-check things."

I kept working on it and went back in time through two to three years of information and unraveled the truth. This was the truth:

- They had not been paying the sales taxes for sales generated by an acquisition made three years before. They were three years overdue with huge penalties and interest looming when it was discovered. It was definitely a bad situation.
- They had been paying, just as they told me, the other sales taxes. However, for two years, they had been paying them by hitting the Income Statement for an expense that wasn't our expense. It was already in the holding place. By not taking it out of the holding place and combining it with the acquisition problem, they were causing the holding

place to grow each month and hurting our income statement. This part of the situation was even worse.

The controller was impressed, and the tax people were embarrassed. I was tasked with talking our way out of the acquisition issue by confessing to the states and quickly paying to avoid penalty fees and interest. This was chalked up to our computer system conversion two years before. This was truly where the tax department got confused, and things had gone wrong.

Less fun was being tasked with talking our auditors through this massive mistake, and the correction needed to be made without getting written up. I also wanted to avoid embarrassing them for missing the mistake for years during their audit. Thankfully, I was successful. We made it through with zero issues and fixed the mistake on our Income Statement benefitting the company greatly. Several good elements came out of this bad situation by seeing it through, rather than waiting for the infamous "someone else" to fix it.

The Weird Enron Field Investment

I was assigned a task of managing accounting for the minority investments of the firm I was working for, and one was pretty odd. It was an investment in Enron Field, the stadium for the Houston Astros. Looking through the documents, some things were clear: we had made a $5 million investment. What was missing? Minor details such as how we would get our money back and how we would know at any given time what the $5 million was worth. Was it worth more or less now? I asked a lot of questions to no avail. I had one theory: perhaps we would get free tickets to games for a number of years, and the value of these could help me do the accounting. Once again, I came up with nothing. Additionally, the CEO of Enron was on our company's Board of Directors. I worked on this for nine months with no answers and what felt like a bad situation.

Meanwhile, the great Internet crash of 2000 had occurred, taking the value of our investments, which were generally in small Internet firms crashing down to earth. I was responsible for managing the accounting and was faced with writing down $1 billion. Yes, billion with a B. *Well*, I thought, *I've been working on this Enron field thing for nine months, and it sounds like a good time to make it vanish.* I wrote it off with the $1 billion and didn't say a word to anyone. The $5 million was only half of 1% of the write-off, and everyone was focused on the big number. Not a word was said for about another year.

The Enron meltdown occurred with all sorts of bad situations occurring, including stock price declines, lay-offs, investigations and, most importantly to this story, the removal of the Enron CEO from our company's Board of Directors. I got a frantic phone call from my boss in the middle of this turmoil asking, "Whatever happened with the Enron Field Investment? Is it still on the books?"

I replied, "No, I wrote it off."

"When did you write it off?" my boss asked.

"About a year ago."

His only response was to say "phew" and hang up the phone. To this day, I don't know exactly what the investment was all about. My instinct was apparently correct to make it go away and have less connection to Enron, a prime example of making the best out of a bad situation.

Be the Kool-Aid Pitcher!

There are a number of ways to manage these situations by driving through brick walls you encounter at work. These actions will help you rise rapidly.

1. Work to get back up from your supervisors. Keep them informed and get their support.
2. Stop and think. Don't be so sure you are correct. You may miss something.
3. Everyone makes mistakes, so work not to embarrass your colleagues.
4. See it through. Put in the extra time necessary for the work without distracting from your core duties.

After all, when you have a job to do, you have to do it right, as the song says. To me, this means making the best out of the bad situations you encounter.

GO AND GRAB YOUR CAPE!

Guy Clark wrote a song called "The Cape," which includes lyrics about believing in your abilities and ignoring disbelievers.[34]

What a good metaphor for stepping out in faith. It is very helpful to have confidence in your skills and use them in a new territory. Good things can happen if you are willing to branch out and use your skills in new and different ways. Trust your cape, and you can fly!

I Am Not Qualified for the Role

Full disclosure: I was a history major by training in college. I was *such* a history major. The only math course I took was statistics, and I took it on a pass/fail basis out of fear of lowering my GPA. I'd been good at math until Mrs. Smith in Algebra II in high school, and the idea of taking another math course terrified me ever since, even though I managed to do well enough on the ACT to get a semester of math credit in college.

Anyway, while going to college, I found my way into management roles at work, utilizing tools like spreadsheets and financial statement analysis. By the time 1994 rolled around, I had expanded beyond the basics and was fairly adept. However, I still had zero formal training in business or finance. I learned completely through on-the-job training. I had taken a lower-paying job in communications to get off the road from a job with 80% travel I'd been doing for a couple of years. After all, with a baby on the way, I would rather be around to see the baby than have more money and not see him.

I heard the sound from my cubicle as Tom exploded in a fit of anger. "That's it—I quit! I've had more than I can take from all of you!" he exclaimed to the Chief Operating Officer as he gathered his personal items, threw his name badge, and started heading out the door. "By the way, if you are looking for a replacement for me, try Robert ... he knows more naturally than anyone I've ever seen!" were the last words he spoke as the door slammed shut.

It turns out they were rather desperate, as the role was responsible for not only providing financial training to new franchisees but also, more importantly, for getting them financed so they could open their locations. In other words, management had an urgent need for a replacement and no time to conduct a true job search that could take weeks or months. They needed someone right then.

It took them about five minutes to come ask me to step into an office. They asked me if I would like the role, and they told me I would have Tom's old office—an upgrade from cubicle-land—the new title of director of accounting and a 12% pay increase. In my head, I said, "I am in no way qualified for this role." Out loud, after giving it ten seconds of thought, I said, "I accept" while expecting some transition time or training.

Instead of meeting my expectations for a transition, they said, "Congratulations! We'll let you move your stuff into the office tonight, and you start full-time in the role tomorrow." So, I drove home after moving my things and went to the Tucson Public Library and checked out some books on finance and accounting and started reading that night. It was a scary time, but I grabbed my cape, and it turned out to be a good move. By the way, after several years, I did return to school to get my MBA with concentrations in finance and information technology. However, this was due to me realizing I couldn't keep relying on my *Accounting the Easy Way* book for my day-to-day finance job or further promotions!

Legally Blind Accountant—Rising Rapidly

Having just received a promotion and a new team, I asked a few questions before meeting them. When I learned Kenneth, the leader of the department, was legally blind, I wondered aloud, "How can you be an accountant and be legally blind? How does it work?" My manager wasn't close to the situation and didn't have an answer. So, I set out to meet the team, including Kenneth, and figure it out for myself.

There's legally blind, as in you can't get a driver's license, and there's legally blind, like Kenneth. I entered his office and all of the lights were turned off. To see the computer screens, he had to have the lights turned off and the screen images reversed so the background was dark and letters were in white. He also had an enlarging machine that allowed him to take paper documents and make them legible. Candidly, my initial impression was I had been handed an HR nightmare that no one wanted to deal with. Seriously, there had to be performance issues, but how in the world do you counsel an employee in this situation to improve? I pictured myself saying, "Ok, Kenneth, I need you to be less blind now." That would not work. Additionally, exiting him from the organization would be a nightmare also.

Surprisingly, Kenneth turned out to be one of the best, if not *the best*, accountants I'd ever worked with in my career. Due to the issues with his sight, he had forced himself to be more efficient than anyone else. He knew shortcuts in software using his keyboard I had never seen before and could get work done impossibly quickly. As his eyesight was steadily degrading, all I had to do was check in with him every six months to get him better equipment, such as a larger monitor for his computer. He had risen through his career by overachieving and finding his way around the obstacles in his way.

Nope—Not Qualified for This One Either!

I was new to the world of consulting—about two-and-a-half weeks new. Happy to have a job, I was learning about as quickly as I could. Officially, I was the first employee for the firm in the U.S. No pressure whatsoever! I was attending my first conference and my boss and bosses' boss (the founder and CEO) came up to me and said they had a potential project opportunity for me. It was with a former client who had years before rejected further consulting but was now coming back and asking for help in the implementation phase of a project.

After I took a quick look at the position overview and specifications, I quickly reached the conclusion I did not *remotely* fit the qualifications the client was looking for in the project. It was practically an alphabet soup of letters—CPA, PMP, Six Sigma Black Belt, CFE—none of which I had. The closest was two days of training that made me a Six Sigma Yellow Belt. I told the CEO my apprehensions, to which he replied, "We've scheduled the interview with the client for 15 minutes from now on Skype. Now, go upstairs to your room, join the interview, and win the work!"

It left me with one path: win the work. I got on the call, and I didn't have to address my lack of qualifications because they had my resume already. Then, I answered their questions and sold them on what I would bring to the job. At the end of the 30-minute call, I walked out of the room having won the work and moved ahead to successfully work on my first consulting project for nine months. I won't say I flew in the words of the song, but I definitely learned how to sell under pressure.

The Lion of the Round Top

You don't picture a college professor with no military training as a likely candidate to rise rapidly to being a major general and Medal of Honor awardee in the Civil War, much less later serving as both the president of a college and state governor. However, Joshua Lawrence Chamberlain proved more capable than anyone other than himself believed.

Joshua Lawrence Chamberlain

Full disclosure: he seems to be a distant relative in my family, but I learned of him far before learning of the possible family connection. As a history major, I learned of his defense of Little Round Top at Gettysburg and the bayonet charge he led that turned the tide of the battle. His battlefield promotion came on his deathbed after an injury, but he forgot he was supposed to die. In fact, he didn't die of his wound until 1914. He participated in Lee's surrender at Appomattox Courthouse, even commanding the troops at the surrender ceremony, and it was supposedly his idea to salute the surrendering troops with honor. He was offered a higher position when he joined the Union Army but stayed humble and declined it as he wanted to learn at a lower level. This learning may have been key to him understanding the strategic position at Gettysburg and the combination of flanking maneuver and charge that turned the tide of the battle.[35]

As a side-note, my great-great-grandfather was also at Gettysburg and was part of the unit tasked with holding the ground on day one of the battle, allowing the other Union troops to retreat and reposition to better ground.

Melvin Cutts Wadsworth (Robert's ancestor)

Those 275 officers and men were told to hold the ground at any cost to allow the 16,000 other troops to retreat. Only 38 men evaded capture, and my great-grandfather was taken prisoner for the rest of the war. However, this action was key to the Union Army having the time to resupply and win the battle.

Both of these leaders showed great impact can be made by learning the details and acting with honor. Chamberlain simply kept rising rapidly even with a wound that never healed and killed him over 48 years later.

Saving Lives in Hong Kong?

I received a call from a friend and former colleague in Hong Kong in December 2019. "I need your help researching best practices in safety and security for a utility company in Hong Kong. They've had a number of deaths, and my company has been hired to recommend areas of improvement." Despite my learnings from past experience, I immediately thought I was not qualified at all for the role. However, my friend needed help. I also realized the income wouldn't be bad, either, in a slow time of the year.

When I started asking questions and participating on conference calls, I only understood about 20% of the discussion. I thought of a good friend who worked in the utility industry in the U.S. and called her. She wasn't the expert but pointed me to someone in operations I could talk with. This helped me ramp up my knowledge quickly and get more comfortable with holding conversations on my own and conducting research. By the end of the six-week project, I had written a fair portion of the report and used some of my technical skills with Adobe Acrobat to produce a good-looking final product.

Burn the Ships

When you think about it, all of us are born unqualified to do much beyond cry and breathe. We have to learn everything else. Certainly, none of us are born experts at anything. So, what can you do when presented a new opportunity? How do you grab your cape and fly?

1. Embrace the fear. You don't need to broadcast you are afraid but don't avoid admitting to yourself you are afraid or unqualified for the role. After all, legend has it that Cortez burned the ships upon arrival, giving his troops the choice to succeed or die during the conquest of Mexico.[36] You don't need to take it that far but keep it in mind.

2. Do a quick pros and cons evaluation. What are the downsides? What are the upsides? What happens if it all goes bad? If the scales tilt toward the pros, as they did with me in a better title, pay, and experience, then take the role.

3. Ramp up your training. Being honest with yourself is critical. After all, one of my favorite authors used to say, "No one can 'get' an **education**, for of necessity **education** is a continuing process." Embrace this and educate yourself on an ongoing basis.

4. Prepare. Are you reading non-fiction books about things you know nothing about? If not, start doing this on an ongoing basis. You never know what the next opportunity might be, so being well rounded will help you grab the next big chance!

TIME TO FLY!

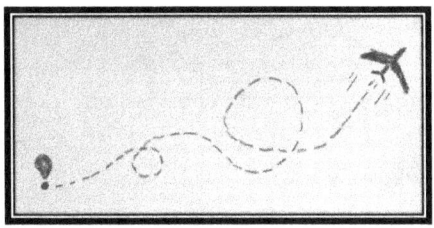

Did you know I used to be able to run faster than Steve Austin, the infamous *Six-Million Dollar Man* from the 1970s TV show? I absolutely remember it being true, and that should count for something! Like any superhero, however, it required a special uniform. At six years old, I dressed in all blue from head to toe—blue shirt and blue jeans. Most importantly, my mom had my blue denim jacket embroidered with a stagecoach on the back and my blue tennis shoes. In the combination, I was "The Blue Bullet!" Able to run around the yard so fast I was a blur!

    I imagine I burned a fair number of calories running around like that every day. My imagination fueled my ability to run really fast, as far as I remember. There were no stop watches, and I probably wasn't very fast, but I didn't know any better and didn't let being realistic stop me. I like to think I still hold a little bit of the mentality in my life in business. Many times, I've wondered if that's one of the reasons I picked a school with blue as one of their primary colors. I'm going to go put on some blue and get some stuff done. It's my equivalent of my cape I trust.

Congratulations on making your through the winding path of a few stories and ideas of how to be the opposite of dumb in your career. You should now be better prepared to grab your cape and find you can fly in your career.

I shared some ideas on the following areas:

Leadership, Not Management, Philosophies
HR Tips HR Might Not Approve Of
Improving the Work in the "Work" Place
Bring on the Dynamite! Removing Obstacles at Work
Rise More Rapidly

For myself, post-surgery, I found myself wanting to do more to contribute positively to society. My recent activities have been focused on helping government and non-governmental organizations improve operations, resulting in both more funding to the core mission of the organizations and adding more value to the world. I've helped a global organization aimed at ending world hunger by 2030, state organizations, public universities, federal groups and local, grass-roots societies since recovering in 2018. That has been my way of rising more rapidly. What is your path?

One option for you to fly is to just use a few nuggets you drew from the book to improve your approach to the workplace. A couple of simple ideas that struck you could help you with a situation you are experiencing. Just using a few that strike you can make a big difference to your effectiveness in your workplace and take you to a new level.

Option two is a bit more comprehensive and involves the following steps:

1. Go back through the book again. Skimming is ok! Have a notebook with you and take some notes when points strike you.
2. Decide on your goal or goals. Is it to solve human resource problems—or to get promoted more rapidly? Maybe it is both.
3. Prioritize which sections you want to address first.
4. Set a target date for the achievement of your goal.
5. Put on your cape and find out you can fly!

APPENDIX

Project Plan Example

Following is a high-level example of a project plan overview:

	2020			
	21-Feb	28-Feb	6-Mar	13-Mar
Location Improvement - Short Term				
1 Joint Meeting & Plan				
1.1 Joint Meeting	■			
1.2 Meeting Output & Project Plan	■			
2 Ergonomics/Safety				
2.1 Farebox Height - Money Rooms		■	■	
2.2 Fixed Route Money Rooms		■	■	
2.3 All Locations		■	■	
3 Build Expertise				
3.1 Daily Audit Sheets		■	■	
3.2 Farebox Placement in Cubicles		■	■	
3.3 Farebox Maintenance Policy		■	■	
4 Reports/Analytics				
4.1 Eliminate Non-Value Adding Reports			■	
4.2 Manifest Mapping			■	
4.3 Reports/Analytics - Monthly			■	
5 IT Systems/Tools				
5.1 Utilization of Excel and Shared Drive			■	■
5.2 Redemption Policy			■	■
6 Pay for Performance/HR				
6.1 Ensure Implementation of Pay for Performance	■	■	■	
6.2 Job Description Modification	■	■	■	
6.3 Organization Chart Modification	■	■	■	
6.4 Staff Management/Communication				
6.5 Policy/Protocol - Rollout				
6.5 Ongoing Monitoring				
7 Project Management				
7.1 Ongoing Reporting	■	■	■	■
7.2 Visit all locations - with Mgt Team	■	■	■	■

Project Stakeholder Chart (Sample)

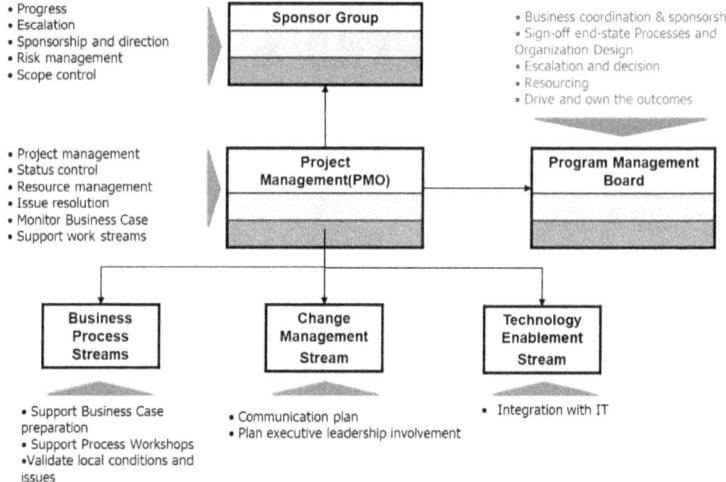

Project Role Definitions (Sample)

Project Sponsor
3 sponsors
(Names)

- Formulates the goal of the program in alignment with the strategy.
- Ensures alignment and management support at the Business Units.
- Responsible for the delivery of the value from the Program.
- Presents Program Business Case and Program Charter to Leadership.
- Appoints Program Steering Committee Members, Business Program Manager, and Project Sponsors for all underlying projects.
- Approves program Business Case, charter, plan, and closure documents as part of the Program Steering Committee.
- Takes decisions on program progress (tollgates) and deviations vs. the plan.

Business Project Manager for the engagement (Name)	<ul><li>Translates the strategic imperatives into specific initiatives and objectives.</li><li>Organizes all business stakeholders to ensure the realization of the program.</li><li>Owns the program Business Case, Program Charter, and Closure documents.</li><li>Presents program status on monthly review meetings.</li><li>Ensures alignment of project objectives with program objectives.</li><li>Provides guidance to project implementation by participation in Project Steering Committees.</li><li>Ensures information on non-related projects is provided to the PMO Program manager to facilitate complete program reporting.</li></ul>

APPENDIX

PMO Program Manager Business Transformation (Name)	<ul><li>Ensures the progress of the Program by employing structured management practices.</li><li>Applies a 'best practice' process and methodology for Program Management.</li><li>Drives the creation of the Program documents: Business Case, Program Charter, Program Closure in collaboration with all stakeholders.</li><li>Ensures timely and consistent reporting for program status reviews and tollgates; facilitates meetings/conference calls related to the program.</li><li>Ensures complete information of the status of all underlying projects to the program team.</li><li>Provides complete information on program status and decisions to the Project Managers.</li></ul>

Weekly Project Update Example

Week Ended February 14, 2020	(Project Name) Project Status Report Internal Lead: [NAME] External Lead: Robert Towle			Overall Status
Key Achievements		**Project Deliverables**	**Date/Status**	
1. Conducted Interview with external agency regarding Case Study on technology and process improvements 2. Benchmarking Information finalization 3. Draft Report Finalization 4. Read-out meeting scheduling		Kick-Off Meeting	1/28/2020	Complete
		Interviews	2/7/2020	Complete
		Additional Questions	2/12/2020	Complete
		Benchmarking Information	2/12/2020	Complete
		Draft Report	2/14/2020	Complete
		Presentation of Findings	2/19/2020	Scheduled
Planned Activities – Week of 2/17/2020 - 2/21/2020		Finalize Report	2/20/2020	Scheduled
1. Presentation in Face-to-Face Meeting in Wilmington (2/19) 2. Draft Report Finalized – with feedback (2/20)				
Risks, Issues, Decisions, Dependencies		**Budget**		
1. Slight delay in report finalization and presentation due to scheduling, meeting now scheduled for 2/19/2020		Time		
		Expenses		

Legend: In Process | Slightly Off Track | Significantly Off Track | Complete | Not Started

APPENDIX

S.T.U.P.I.D. Sighting Report

S.T.U.P.I.D.

Sighting Report

Date:

Name:

Brief Description:

Detailed Description:

Ideas to Resolve:

ENDNOTES

1. "Seeing the Elephant," October 4, 2020. https://en.wikipedia.org/wiki/Seeing_the_elephant.
2. "I've Been Everywhere." Johnny Cash Official Site, July 29, 2019. https://www.johnnycash.com/track/ive-been-everywhere-6/.
3. "Johnny Cash And The Tennessee Three - One Piece At A Time." Discogs, January 1, 1976. https://www.discogs.com/Johnny-Cash-And-The-Tennessee-Three-One-Piece-At-A-Time/release/1562660.
4. "Mr. and Mrs. Lester Hough Celebrate Golden Wedding Anniversary June 26." Randleman Reporter, July 12, 1989.
5. "You Can't Always Get What You Want — The Rolling Stones ..." Accessed October 26, 2020. https://www.last.fm/music/The+Rolling+Stones/_/You+Can%27t+Always+Get+What+You+Want.
6. Gomes, Whitney Z. "I Want You to Want Me - Cheap Trick: Songs, Reviews, Credits." AllMusic. Accessed October 26, 2020. https://www.allmusic.com/album/i-want-you-to-want-me-mw0000078895.
7. Ruhlmann, William. "Running on Empty - Jackson Browne: Songs, Reviews, Credits." AllMusic. Accessed October 26, 2020. https://www.allmusic.com/album/running-on-empty-mw0000193103.
8. "History of the Eagles (2013)." History of the Eagles (2013) directed by Alison Ellwood • Reviews, film + cast • Letterboxd. Accessed October 26, 2020. https://letterboxd.com/film/history-of-the-eagles/.

9. Goodwin, Doris Kearns. Team of Rivals: the Political Genius of Abraham Lincoln. New York: Simon & Schuster Paperbacks, 2012.
10. "Say Goodbye To Hollywood." Billy Joel Official Site, February 17, 2016. https://www.billyjoel.com/song/say-goodbye-hollywood-8/.
11. Craig, David. "The Hampton Witch." Lane Memorial Library. Accessed October 26, 2020. http://www.hampton.lib.nh.us/hampton/biog/thehamptonwitch.htm.
12. "What Are the Scout Oath and Scout Law?" Boy Scouts of America, December 16, 2019. https://www.scouting.org/about/faq/question10/.
13. "The Brady Gang." FBI. FBI, May 18, 2016. https://www.fbi.gov/history/famous-cases/the-brady-gang.
14. "Already Gone — Eagles | Last.fm." Accessed October 26, 2020. https://www.last.fm/music/Eagles/_/Already+Gone.
15. "Huey Lewis And The News* - Jacob's Ladder." Discogs, January 1, 1986. https://www.discogs.com/Huey-Lewis-And-The-News-Jacobs-Ladder/release/3558804.
16. by, Posted, and Mqs. "Boston – Boston (1976) [SACD 2000] {SACD ISO + FLAC 24bit/88,2kHz}." MQS Albums Download, January 20, 2018. https://mqs.link/boston-boston-1976-sacd-2000-sacd-iso-flac-24bit882khz/.
17. Lundin, Stephen C., John Christensen, Harry Paul, and Kenneth H. Blanchard. Fish!: a Proven Way to Boost Morale and Improve Results. New York: Hachette Books, 2020.
18. "Workin' at the Car Wash Blues - Jim Croce: Song Info." AllMusic. Accessed October 26, 2020. https://www.allmusic.com/song/workin-at-the-car-wash-blues-mt0002622996.

[19] "Dire Straits: Money for Nothing." IMDb. IMDb.com. Accessed October 26, 2020. https://www.imdb.com/title/tt4645630/.

[20] Daily, Founder of Charleston, Author Founder of Charleston Daily, Founder of Charleston Daily, Matt Rhoney says: Founder of Charleston Daily says: Evy says: Skateboard News Says: Super Crispy Taco says: and Robert M says: "Weird South Carolina Laws and Statutes Past and Present." Charleston Daily, July 16, 2017. https://charlestondaily.net/weird-south-carolina-laws/.

[21] "Pressure." Billy Joel Official Site, February 17, 2016. https://www.billyjoel.com/song/pressure-7/.

[22] bobbiejean87@gmail.com. "'Landslide': The Story Behind the 1975 Fleetwood Mac Classic and The Chicks' Country Cover." Wide Open Country, July 7, 2020. https://www.wideopencountry.com/landslide-dixie-chicks/.

[23] The biography of W. Edwards Deming. Accessed October 26, 2020. http://www.fr-deming.org/whoised.html.

[24] "Fool in the Rain — Led Zeppelin | Last.fm." Accessed October 26, 2020. https://www.last.fm/music/Led+Zeppelin/_/Fool+in+the+Rain.

[25] "Statistician's Blues, by Todd Snider." Todd Snider, December 11, 2009. https://toddsnider.bandcamp.com/track/statisticians-blues?action=download.

[26] "Stranger in Town (Album) - WikiMili, The Free Encyclopedia." WikiMili.com. Accessed October 26, 2020. https://wikimili.com/en/Stranger_in_Town_(album).

[27] "Chaff." Merriam-Webster. Merriam-Webster. Accessed October 26, 2020. https://www.merriam-webster.com/dictionary/chaff.

[28] "The Weight — The Band - Last.fm | Play Music, Find Songs ..." Accessed October 26, 2020. https://www.last.fm/music/The+Band/Music+From+Big+Pink+(Remastered)/The+Weight.

29. "Getting Better." Wikipedia. Wikimedia Foundation, October 23, 2020. https://en.wikipedia.org/wiki/Getting_Better.
30. "David Allen Coe - You Never Even Called Me By My Name Lyrics." SongMeanings. Accessed October 26, 2020. https://songmeanings.com/songs/view/89501/.
31. Sage, Jerry. Sage: the Man the Nazis Couldn't Hold. New York: Dell Pub. Co., 1985.
32. "Billy Joel – I Go to Extremes." Genius, October 17, 1989. https://genius.com/Billy-joel-i-go-to-extremes-lyrics.
33. "Live And Let Die (Song)." The Paul McCartney project, October 29, 2018. https://www.the-paulmccartney-project.com/song/live-and-let-die/.
34. "Guy Clark – The Cape." Genius, April 4, 1995. https://genius.com/Guy-clark-the-cape-lyrics.
35. Chamberlain, Joshua Lawrence. The Passing of the Armies: an Account of the Final Campaign of the Army of the Potomac, Based upon Personal Reminiscences of the Fifth Army Corps. Charleston, SC: Nabu Press, 2012.
36. "Cortes Burns His Boats", The Fall of the Aztecs, Wood, Michael. Conquistadors. London: BBC Digital, 2015.

ABOUT THE AUTHOR

Robert was born in North Carolina and lived throughout the U.S and in (West) Germany during his childhood, including going to three schools between 9th and 12th grade. He gained a strong interest for both history and traveling due to his experiences and went to Southwestern University in Georgetown, Texas, for his BA in history. As a side note, with no offense to Baylor graduates, Southwestern is absolutely the oldest university in Texas being founded in 1840 while Texas was still a republic.

He has lived in Texas four different times and in eight different towns in the state. Since graduation, he has worked at different companies in Arizona, Texas, New Jersey, and Virginia. He went back to school and got his MBA with concentrations in finance and IT from Auburn University in Alabama in 2000. Although the majority of his career has been in finance and consulting, he has also worked as a bicycle mechanic, caterer, dishwasher, optical technician, apartment manager, and communications coordinator. He migrated from traditional finance roles, including vice president of finance and CFO roles, into being a consultant in 2013. Since then, he has worked with a wide variety of clients including the U.S. Department of Health and Human Services, Panasonic, the Iowa University System, University of California-Davis, First Data (now Fiserv), and the International Baccalaureate, traveling to Singapore, Hong Kong, Macau, Sri Lanka, France, Colombia, Mexico, the UK, and Poland for his work.

He moved out on his own in 2018 by forming his own company, 636 Advisors, to continue to help both small and large clients. He is also working with PrimCorp, LLC is an award-winning SBA 8(a) certified and Service-Disabled Veteran Owned Small Business (SDVOSB) management consulting company with a U.S. Federal Agency. In his free time, he continues to practice guitar and other instruments and has been working some singing and playing into training sessions for various business topics. Genealogy is another of his hobbies through which he's found he's distantly related to authors Henry Wadsworth Longfellow and Louis L'Amour.

Robert has testified before a sub-committee of the U.S. House of Representatives on Shared Services as well as serving on the Joint Commission to improve the connection between Radford University and the City of Radford, Virginia. He lives with his wife in Southwest Virginia in the heart of the New River Valley. Opinions vary over how a river this far west got a name like New River, but the prevailing theory says it was originally left off a map and added later. Another point of trivia is the river runs north, which is fairly rare for rivers for some reason he doesn't understand, but he plans to figure it out someday.

Free Online Assessment & Spotify Playlist

Answer a 10-question survey for a free Spotify playlist of the songs in *Don't Be Dumb* and a summary of areas in which you would benefit from further leadership coaching.

Go to www.636Advisors.com for your online survey.

Robert M. Towle

BRING **R**OBERT TO YOUR NEXT EVENT

DON'T **B**E **D**UMB
Robert is a proven speaker at national and international events and provide interactive workshops to improve your workspace.

Start the conversation today.
Robert@636Advisors.com

Interactive Training Sessions

Three-hour on-site interactive training sessions or webinars focused on the needs of your organization. Topics include:

- Putting Your Business on the Path to Recovery through Business Planning
- Propelling Your Business Through Creating a Great Customer Experience
- Raising Stakeholder Engagement

One- to two-day on-site interactive training sessions.
Topics include

- Stakeholder Engagement Approach—including the following topics

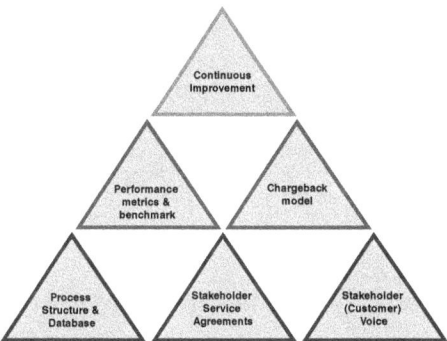

Complimentary Conversation

One-hour phone or video discussion about your needs and opportunities to improve in your business

Ongoing Coaching Calls

One to four hours per month to discuss business results, objectives, challenges, and next steps

Business Plan Development

Business Transformation Projects

Experience in leading business transformation in a variety of areas:

- Small Business Start-up—Proven Program to cut break-even times in half
- Software Implementation—how to harness the power of technology to improve your business
- Process Improvements

Get the conversation starting by emailing Robert@636Advisors.com

www.ingramcontent.com/pod-product-compliance
Lightning Source LLC
LaVergne TN
LVHW012102070526
838200LV00074BA/3921